stick•y *(stik′ē)* *adj.*   **1** The message that holds fast, adheres, and clings to the heart of every generation. **2** Eternal content independent of time, change, and cyberspace.

@stickyJesus™

how to live out your faith online

Toni Birdsong   Tami Heim

Abingdon Press
Nashville

@stickyjesus
how to live out your faith online

Digital Scribe Press, P.O. Box 9129, Gallatin, TN 37066, Email: info@digitalscribepress.com

Library of Congress Cataloging-in-Publication Data

Birdsong, Toni.

@stickyjesus : how to live out your faith online / Toni Birdsong, Tami Heim.

p. cm.

Includes bibliographical references (p.).

ISBN 978-1-4267-4189-0 (book - hardback with printed dust jacket : alk. paper) 1. Christian life—Meditations. 2. Jesus Christ—Meditations. I. Heim, Tami. II. Title. III. Title: Stickyjesus.

BV4501.3.B4975 2012

248.40285'4678—dc23

2011044377

Toni Birdsong, Tami Heim

Printed in the United States of America
First printing 2010

Cover design by Dual Identity
Interior design by Birdsong Creative, Inc. // Franklin, TN // www.birdsongcreative.com
Photographs of authors by Erin McCaffrey // www.mccaffreyphotography.com

11 12 13 14 15 16 17 18 19 20—10 9 8 7 6 5 4 3 2 1

For J. C.

The Only Famous One

"His dominion is an eternal dominion;
His kingdom endures from generation to generation."
Daniel 4:34, NIV

endorsements

I loved @stickyJesus. It's a must-read for anyone who wants to better understand how to use the massive platform of social media to communicate the hope of Jesus Christ in today's world. Toni Birdsong and Tami Heim obviously know their stuff and you will too if you take the time to digest this incredible tool they've put together.

Pete Wilson
Senior Pastor, Cross Point Church, Nashville, Tennessee
Author, *Plan B*

The new communication technologies of the past two decades have shrunk our world. With so many ways of staying connected that were previously unimaginable, Toni and Tami show us how to engage the world online for Christ. While nothing takes the place of face-to-face relationship, I was excited to read @stickyJesus as it opened up a whole world of possibilities and it's written by authors who are savvy in the field of communication.

Rebecca Pippert
Founder, Salt Shaker Ministries
Best-Selling Author, *Out of the Salt Shaker*

Learn how to express your faith online and reach more people than you ever imagined. This book blew me away.

Ken Blanchard
Best-Selling Coauthor of *The One Minute Manager*
and *Lead Like Jesus*

This book is about love in action, giving practical advice about how to change a world, and be 'in' yet not 'of' it. I learned from this work, and I know you will too.

Laurie Beth Jones
Best-Selling Author of *Jesus CEO; The Path* and *Jesus, Career Counselor*

Church leaders are getting a vision for the power of the Internet and social media to advance their reach both inside and outside the church. @stickyJesus is the first book of its kind to guide Christ followers and equip them to be effective online in their circles of influence. This book keeps it real, focuses on the heart, and inspires each of us to make a difference on this new mission field.

Greg Ligon
Vice President and Publisher, Leadership Network

@stickyJesus is a must-read for every believer born to this age when the world is literally at our fingertips. This book challenges us to be intentional about engaging the world online—not for the building up of ourselves, but for the building up of the Kingdom. @stickyJesus will sharpen your focus, move you to self-examination, and motivate you to interact online in a whole new sticky way. I loved this book. I needed this book!

Kim Cash Tate
Speaker, Women of Faith
Author, *Faithful*

When I first saw the title, @stickyJesus, I had no idea what to expect! I was delighted to discover a book filled with profound truth and practical applications. This book is a Christian's field guide for how to use social media to advance the gospel. As the founder of Women in Christian Media, I believe this is a must-read for all Christian media professionals, as well as for every believer who wants to use social media platforms to reach the world for Christ.

Suellen Roberts
Founder & President, Women in Christian Media

Imagine if we lived at a hinge in history when ordinary people like you could be mobilized as witnesses—as if Jesus Himself were making new nets for many to fish with? Toni and Tami make the convincing case that this is no fantasy. And they are savvy, credible, and flat-out devoted-to-Jesus witnesses, perfectly suited to help us humbly bear the transforming presence of Jesus into this new, networked place called the Internet.

Ken Wilson
Senior Pastor, Vineyard Church, Ann Arbor, Michigan
Author, *Mystically Wired: Exploring New Realms in Prayer*

Jesus said that when the Holy Spirit had come upon us we would be His witnesses to Jerusalem, in all Judea and Samaria and to the ends of the earth (Acts 1:8). The Internet and the exponential growth of social media is the new "ends of the earth." Toni and Tami's clear and readable new book, @stickyJesus, is the Christian handbook for understanding how best to navigate this new place.

Rev. Fr. James Coles
Pastor, St. Ignatius of Antioch Antiochian Orthodox Christian Church, Mesa, Arizona

The world we live in has changed. The days of sitting on the front porch with our neighbors are mostly over and a new day of Tweeting, Facebook, and texting has arrived. We can resist culture all we want but it is the world in which we live. How will the church respond? Authors Toni Birdsong and Tami Heim want to help the church navigate through the challenges of social media with their new book @stickyJesus. This is a helpful and thought-changing book with the potential to help pastors and church leaders become more Kingdom-minded and achieve greater results in reaching people for Christ.

Ron Edmondson
Co-Pastor, Grace Community Church, Clarksville, Tennessee

This book had me from page one—I could not put it down! The new Roman Road is indeed at our fingertips and its reach is incredible. @stickyJesus will compel you to go from observing the social media phenomenon at hand to boldly injecting Christ into the midst of it and radically changing the eternal conversation.

Wade Mikels
Senior Pastor, Village Church, Burbank, California

As a ministry leader I am always looking for new ways to show and share the saving power of Jesus Christ. @stickyJesus has opened my mind and heart to all that God is making possible through social media. We were born for such a time as this and this is our chance to claim the World Wide Web for the glory of God.

Robin M. Bertram
Founder, Robin Bertram Ministries

The widespread ways we as human beings create to connect with one another points to our deep need for relationship. @stickyJesus provides a roadmap for helping believers navigate the online environment in a way that helps build relationships that point to a relationship with God. This is relationship evangelism for a new place and a new time!

Dwayne Reece
Vice President and General Manager, Community Chaplains of America

This book explores the new frontier of "techno-evangelism." People are scrambling to be relevant with trendy Websites, podcasts, blogs, and online tithing. Leveraging technology to reach the virtual mission field enables a believer to share the gospel instantly. @stickyJesus provides great insight on how to be intentional for Christ in our online communities.

Celeste LaReau
Founder & President, Tennessee Christian Chamber of Commerce

file feed

acknowledgments

Toni thanks...

To Troy Birdsong, you are the string on my balloon and proof that God wants me to love deep and sweet on this side of heaven. I'd choose you over and over again and over again. Thank you for being my hero.

To my parents, Ed and Georgia Page, thank you for your unconditional love, steadfast faith, and the gift of laughter. I appreciate that my life is a beautiful quilt and not a finely tailored piece of linen. I love you beyond words.

To my children Zane and Olivia. Thank you for being patient in having a writer for a mom. You are my deepest wells of inspiration and two of the most creative people I know. Your laughter and love carry me through the late nights. I love you to the far side of the Milky Way.

To my brothers Rob and Michael Page. You make me better. Your love (and whoopins) has made me a resilient woman of God. I'm proud to call you two of my very best friends. I pray your adventures never end and that your love of God trumps every other pursuit. I'm so very proud of you both.

To my West Coast pastor, Wade Mikels (Village Church, Burbank). Thank you for "bringing me up" in God's truth, showing me the meaning of "familia," and making the study of God's Word the insatiable pursuit of my life. You are passion and excellence with a pulpit, and an inspiration to so many.

To my Tennessee pastor Steve Berger (Grace Chapel, Leiper's Fork). Thank you for being faithful, digging deep, and living out an uncompromised faith. You are my touchstone for *keeping it real* and serving God with everything I've got...on earth as I will in heaven.

To my Aunt Evelyn and Uncle Frank Kenyon—now beaming residents of heaven. Thank you for taking the time to sit with me and introduce me to Jesus at the tender age of nine. It mattered.

To my unbreakable sisterhood of girlfriends in California and Tennessee—you know *exactly* who you are. You've cheered me on, prayed me up, and kept me focused on what matters. I love you deep.

To Tami Heim. Wow. Thank you for believing God. You are my friend, my sister, my mentor, and the most amazing collaborative partner God could have given me. It's been my pure joy to go white water rafting with you. Is it Friday yet? \0/

And last—but certainly not least—to my Savior, Healer, and Truth-Revealer, Jesus Christ. You are so very kind to me. Thank You for Your awesome love and sweet communion...may my life be a never-ending thank you note back to You.

Tami thanks...

How could I do a book like this and not return the glory to the only place the glory belongs? To God, for relentlessly loving me, saving me, and rewriting the text of my life when I opened the book of my heart to Your eyes. I am grateful that You lead me in the most extraordinary ways. You not only rock my world—You are my all in all.

To my best friend and husband, Dale, thanks for lavishly loving and supporting me over these past thirty-six years of life. Your faithfulness to love me, as Christ loves church and gave His life for it, has drenched my life with fullness and the fire to stand with you as a witness until He comes again.

To my daughter, Zoë, and her husband, Matt, I am grateful for your encouragement and for the many hours you listened to me go on and on and on about what God is making possible *in such a time as this*. You could not bring me any greater joy as I watch you whole-heartedly follow the God-sized plan for your lives. You inspire me.

Mom, Dad, and George—oh yes, I hear you cheering me on from

on high. All three of you always liked the front row of the bleachers. Katherine, thank you for everything you are and for always being a remarkable Mother-in-Law to me.

To ALL the spiritual leaders in my life—thank you. I want to specifically acknowledge Sister Rita for teaching me Freshman English and making it perfectly clear that the only reason or purpose for my life was to know, love, and serve God. To Pastor Ken and Nancy Wilson, thanks for living authentic faith and being indescribably lovely. To Pastor David Landrith, thanks not only for how you shepherd my soul and shower me with truth, but also for using Twitter to connect my heart to a completely infectious crazy love in Jeremie, Haiti. In 140 characters you first took me to Haiti to find Johnny's family and now after all that has followed, my life will never be the same.

I must extend a special helping of gratitude to my dear friend, Lisa Rollins, and my pup, Kali. If it were not for the two of you—I might, just might, have missed Facebook.

To Mike Hyatt, the thank you list for you includes a thousand things, but on this occasion thank you for leading me to the point of WOW, where geek and God intersect.

To Toni—thanks for your obedience, willing heart, and tireless passion. You are a testimony to the power of a single tweet and how God always dreams bigger dreams for our lives than we possibly could. \0/

And to all the people that God has put in my life—yes, all of you—thank you for leaving fingerprints on my being and letting God use you to stretch the size of my heart from here to the ends of the earth for His glory.

Tami & Toni thank...

To the team at Birdsong Creative—Troy Birdsong, Matt Green, Ai Nguyen, Todd Lyda, and David Calhoun. Thank you for your ingenuity and commitment, and for putting wings on a very precious thing. To Maurilio Amorim and Shannon Litton—for your friendship, counsel, and support. Thanks for supplying lots of laughter when we needed it the most.

To the team at Abingdon Press (United Methodist Publishing House). Thank you for your vision on this project and for using your influence in this world to equip others to #LiveSticky in the online world for Jesus Christ.

To Dale Heim for letting us camp out over these many months and for resisting changing the locks. You kept the coffee flowing and blessed us with a consistent stream of inspiration, generosity, and kindness. We love you (and Kali girl) for sticking with us.

To Dimples Kellogg, our exceptional copyeditor, and our eagle-eyed proofreaders Carrie Marrs and Kevin Harvey. It takes a village of passionate perfectionists to tame a manuscript—and our village rocked. Thank you all.

To our Women in Christian Media (WCM) sisterhood. Your awakened hearts, encouragement, and fire for the gospel spur us on.

To Amy Parker for angel prayers that carried us and for being a loyal colleague, sister, and friend.

To our Facebook and Twitter friends (we do call you friends). Thank you for #keepingitreal, inspiring us daily to record (and echo) God's movement online, and for living out your faith so passionately for team Jesus. A special thanks to those who opened their hearts and shared their sticky stories of courage, compassion, and hope in these pages. You are Digital Scribes™—true pioneers—for the Kingdom. It's our honor and joy to #LiveSticky with you daily and light up the online space in His name, for His fame.

introduction: what's sticky got to do with it?

> **@stickyJesus** My message clings to people's hearts—forever.

Hey! Just wanted to share a quick note with you...since we've become Facebook friends I really look to you for inspiration. I have been through a lot in the last three years. Some days are better than others. When I read your posts I realize that life is a journey and God has a plan. Some days I actually feel like He is working through you to talk to me. Anyway, I did something crazy tonight...I found a church with a ladies' Bible study near my house and actually went! I feel really, really good. Actually, I can't wait to go back. I can't explain it. I wanted you to be the first to know.

This post, sent to us from our Facebook friend Melissa Paolo-Corcoran, is just one of the thirty *billion* pieces of content exchanged on Facebook each month by the seven hundred fifty million people (to date) now connecting daily on the largest social networking site on the planet.

The sheer volume of human connection and conversation taking place on social networking sites daily is mind-blowing. But what's more awesome is that at the heart of the digital note you just read is the *sticky* love of Jesus Christ.

Sticky. It means different things to different people. To marketers, sticky is the Holy Grail, what it's all about. It's the secret sauce in an advertising message that helps it hit the mark, get attention, and move people to act. A "sticky message" stays around longer than most.

But we define sticky in a whole new way—a way that relates to Jesus and His message. Sticky holds fast, adheres, and clings to the heart of every generation. Sticky is an eternal message independent of time, change, and cyberspace. It's the supernatural movement of God unaffected by Wi-Fi, bandwidth, or gigabytes. A sticky message is unyielding to cultural fodder or trends. It's a holy whisper in a noisy land.

Of all the messages the world has ever heard, the gospel is still the stickiest. The good news is that God's message is *your* message, which makes your presence and voice online wholly (and holy) indispensable!

This book is for every Christ follower residing on this side of heaven. It's for those who realize—and those who have yet to understand—the awesome moment into which we've been born. It's for technology novices, casual surfers, and those already folded comfortably into the online world.

Wherever you are in your skill level, it's time to direct your heart toward the sticky things of God.

We challenge you as a Christ follower to change your mind-set of the way you spend your time online. We challenge believers around the world to forgo denomination, sit in the same pew, and write this ongoing story *together* and share new ways to reach a fragmented world for Christ.

Together, we can light up the online space. We can "go" and we can "tell" as Jesus asked each of us to do. And we can change absolutely *everything*.

Changing the world doesn't begin with knowing technology; it begins with knowing Christ. In *Sticky Jesus* we will equip you for the online world by looking to the Equipper, Jesus. We will show you how He connected, created community, and ignited a buzz the world has yet to replicate. We will look at His character, His process, and His priorities and how you can echo His heart online.

In these pages we will do the following:

✓ Explore how Christ honored and built relationships and how you can do the same online.

✓ Give you a practical understanding of the marketing-driven culture online.

✓ Point to the Holy Spirit as your Power Source.

- ✓ Provide personal stories that show God moving and transforming lives through social networking channels.

- ✓ Summarize each file with a download and a prayer that are 100 percent retweetable.

- ✓ Alert you to the danger zones.

- ✓ Demystify the world of social networking with easy instruction on getting started on Facebook, Twitter, blogging, and content gathering (RSS).

- ✓ Provide ongoing resources to help you grow beyond this book at http://www.stickyjesus.com/.

- ✓ Include a glossary in the back of the book to help you along the way.

So who are we to author this book? We are professional communicators by trade and passionate practitioners of all things social media. More importantly, we are Christ followers who understand the power of the gospel and how it can radically change the game online if—*and only if*—we get in the game. And by the way, God connected our two hearts through the power of a single tweet.

We've seen the amazing, eternal fruit that honestly sharing our lives with others—and listening—online produces. So, we've stepped off-line to share that knowledge with you.

Pssst! We'd also like to let you in on a little secret: if we can do this, so can you!

Yes, the online culture is full of strange language (Plaxo, Google+, Twitter, Flickr, YouTube, and the like). But don't let that scare you. This is easy stuff. Really easy. And we'll prove it.

Take up your charge, believer. This is your time. You are the light of the world. God has entrusted you with circles of influence online filled with people—all kinds of people—whom He loves deeply. We pray that you grow in your desire to know Christ and explore the special way He's calling you to shine in this new digital land. So, let's get started—together.

you: born for such a time as this

> **@stickyJesus** The land is shiny, but you are My light.

Share

Welcome to the Land of Shiny Things. Your citizenship was not overtly solicited, but gradually you made your way here. You are an unwitting but active, dues-paying resident. The Land of Shiny Things is a finely manicured mental, spiritual, and physical subdivision of our universal domain. It is the cookie-cutter context that wraps itself around your mind daily, and for lack of an intuitive escape route, you fall into it...way too easily.

The Land of Shiny Things begins to define itself when you hit the snooze on the digital alarm in the morning. Without waking up fully you point the remote at the television, and an impersonal, albeit strangely comforting hum paints a layer over the room...and over your thoughts.

The morning sun rises in supernatural splendor but fails to compete with the shiny box that has reeled in your gaze. Your need to know far outweighs your need for much else. Amid the stream of shiny things coursing through your mind, you hope to catch a glimpse or deduct a rational prediction, based on your library of shiny apps, reliable resources, and mobile reports, of what the unopened day ahead might hold. The shiny coffeepot is programmed to perk. You punch the shiny toaster and poke the shiny blender. You pet your shiny dog that now has a shiny chip surgically implanted so he can't get lost in the Land of Shiny Things.

You kiss your shiny kids good-bye as they get on a bus where all the shiny kids blindly slide into their seats, careful not to interrupt an intense texting tango, blowing out the next game level, or snagging a hot song download.

Rather than swap stories or baseball cards, they peer into their shiny Game Boys, PSPs, cell phones, and iPods.

Meanwhile, you get in your shiny car, complete with a shiny GPS that gives you a 0.2 percent margin of error that you will make it to your destination within 0.6 percent of the estimated time without wasting a moment on a wrong turn or inefficient route. Stop! Go back! You almost left your shiny cell phone, which would render you unreachable and unconnected—the equivalent of being among society's electronically disabled.

At the office you ache to skip the pleasantries. Cordial people move soooo slowly, you think. Chitchat and office banter exist to delay the euphoric cliff dive into the shiny stream of e-mails and other online destinations corralled on the other side of your shiny laptop screen. Ahhhhhh! Finally one with the Wi-Fi, you are officially powered up and a contributor to a world fueled by batteries, power cords, and chargers. You are persuaded of your unique presence as you join the other 2 billion people on the planet who inhabit the Internet daily.[1]

You need to know and be known, and there's little room for God in this shiny equation.

what time is it anyway?

We live in a time when information and the access to it are more powerful than ever. Armed with the right content (information), you become (or feel) more in control of the world around you. The right information helps you make better decisions about how to live, interact, and succeed. You seek information to help with purchasing, investing, staying healthy, being successful in a career, parenting, traveling, buying real estate, maintaining relationships, voting, eating, doing business, and if you're on such a quest...finding God.

Google has wooed the world. But who woos the hearts of men and women? The Bible says the Holy Spirit. But these days it's easier to get more personal with Google than with God and other people. Increasingly, people search Google for information about personal issues such as marriage, depression, parenting, addiction, finances, disease, sexuality, loneliness, and eating disorders. And people do it often without a thought of reaching out to one another or to God.

Has Google replaced the belief that God is omnipresent and all-knowing, and can even answer prayers? As absurd as it may sound, a generation that has grown up as digital natives communicating in real time via instant messages might shock you with a resounding "yes."

Christians are just as immersed in digital technologies and social networks as anyone else.

Relax. There's no need to renounce your residency in the Land of Shiny Things or mask the evidence of your connected life. There's no shame. This is the hour to which you've been born—so by all means, power up! Just power up the way God wants you to. That means with a God-breathed strategy, Holy Spirit power, and divine discernment.

A 2008 study by George Barna indicates that matters of faith play a small role in differentiating people's technological habits. The study found that Christians are just as immersed in (and dependent on) digital technologies and social networks as anyone else. Christians emerged as statistically "on par" with national norms.

David Kinnaman, the lead researcher on the project, gives the research context and warns church leaders to strike a balance between the spiritual and the cultural potential of today's technology. While technology allows us to reach the masses, it's no substitute for the human impact of life-on-life discipleship, says Kinnaman. He adds, "whether or not you welcome it, technology creates an entirely new calculus of influence and independence. The stewardship of technology as a force for good in culture is an important role for technologists, entrepreneurs, educators, and Christian leaders."[2]

For you, a Christ follower, the discussion around technology and its impact for good cannot be left to chance. It's a conversation that must be an ongoing priority. It must become part of the writings, readings, and teachings that communicate faith to this and future generations. And if businesses, motivated by profitability and survival, continue to generate effective content marketing solutions and new ways to engage the public, the body of Christ should be alert—and teachable—to use those same strategies.

How much more critical is the message of salvation than communicating the benefits of the latest fat-free soup or the faster running shoe? *Exactly*.

We live and communicate in awesome times. And we live in one of *the most exciting* windows for sharing the gospel since the Gutenberg press was invented in 1440, making Bibles accessible to the masses.

Until that time books, including the Bible, were painstakingly copied by hand and available only to the wealthiest and most educated people. German-born Johannes Gutenberg died without knowing that his invention would spark the Renaissance, the Industrial Revolution, and the Reformation and catapult the spread of Christianity.

Multiple media, including literature, art, television, film, and radio, have collectively transmitted the gospel message over time. Although their impact has been great, nothing can compare to the mind-blowing—and ever-evolving—impact of the Internet, namely, the content-sharing side called Web 2.0 and the spin-off industry of (and obsession with) social networking. No doubt, a monumental shift is taking place around the world politically, socially, and economically. Social networking is consuming the collective psyche and redefining the understanding of words as traditional as *community* and *friends*.

a snapshot of influence

The speed of change and the numbers are staggering when you consider what is happening around you. Perhaps you are familiar with some of these statistics.[3] If not, be prepared to have your thinking rocked.

❖ It took radio thirty-eight years to reach fifty million users; television, thirteen years; the Internet, four years; and the iPod, three years. In just a nine-month period, Facebook added one hundred million users, and downloads of iPhone applications reached one billion. (That's billion with a *b*.)

❖ Print newspaper circulation is down seven million over the last twenty-five years. But in the last five years, unique readers of online newspapers have increased thirty million.

❖ Collectively, the television networks ABC, NBC, and CBS get ten million unique visitors every month, and these businesses have been around for a combined two hundred years. YouTube, Facebook, and MySpace got 250 million unique visitors each month after being launched for only six years.

❖ In 2008, Barack Obama leveraged online social networks to raise $500 million and mobilized young voters via social networking at unprecedented numbers. He outpaced opponent John McCain in fundraising online by five times.[4]

- Ninety-six percent of people born between 1980 and 1994 have joined a social network.

- Nielsen research reveals that Americans spend a quarter of their time online; a third of that time is spent communicating across social networks, blogs, personal e-mail, and instant messaging. The world now spends over 110 billion minutes on social networks and blog sites.

- One out of every five couples married in the U.S. met via social networking.

Still think using social media is a fad or a waste of time? You may soon join the ranks of these leading, albeit well-meaning, thinkers:[5]

"Everyone acquainted with the subject will recognize it as a conspicuous failure."

—Henry Morton, president of the Stevens Institute of Technology,
on Thomas Edison's light bulb, 1880

"We have reached the limits of what is possible with computers."

—John von Neumann,
infamous mathematician and pioneer of quantum mechanics, 1949

"The horse is here to stay but the automobile is only a novelty— a fad."

—The president of the Michigan Savings Bank
advising Henry Ford's lawyer not to invest in the Ford Motor Co., 1903

"Remote shopping, while entirely feasible, will flop—because women like to get out of the house, like to handle merchandise, like to be able to change their minds."

—Time, 1966

"While theoretically and technically television may be feasible, commercially and financially it is an impossibility, a development of which we need waste little time dreaming."

—Lee DeForest,
American radio pioneer and inventor of the vacuum tube, 1926

"Transmission of documents via telephone wires is possible in principle, but the apparatus required is so expensive that it will never become a practical proposition."

—Dennis Gabor, British physicist, 196

what does it all mean?

It means anyone with an imperative message to communicate has to think bigger. People are migrating online. And as they continue to build niche communities, a significant window is open that should have every person who is concerned with the things of Christ sitting upright and being fully engaged.

The Web has a culture all its own.

This dramatic shift in communication and the growing hunger for human connection online have spawned a new mission field unlike any the church has ever seen.

This mission field has a language and culture all its own. You haven't trained for it. You're not exactly sure how it works. Its velocity can be intimidating. The reference books and mission training programs tailored to impact a Web-based world...well, they simply don't exist.

You stand here as a Christ follower in a definitive moment in time; you are an ordinary person called to usher a holy Kingdom into an increasingly fragmented world. It's the perfect scenario for God to move in big ways, just as He always has. Just as God called Esther, Joseph, and Paul to go before the world's kings at appointed times to alter history, He now calls you to log on and upload what's critical to today's conversation.

While everything changes at warp speed, the holy mandate remains: to communicate the gospel in the most relevant channels available here, there, and everywhere...even if "everywhere" includes foreign lands with peculiar names like Twitter, Facebook, Google, and Plaxo.

the lay of the land

What does this new mission field look like, and who dwells there? It's unique, a place where increasingly "connected" people can easily become more spiritually disconnected. Amid the urban sprawl of technology, they congregate, shop, work, share, play, and live online. It's a shiny terrain, indeed.

In *The World Is Flat*, author Thomas L. Friedman asserts that there's no turning back from this "mobile me" era; that the cheap availability of software and broadband Internet has leveled the global landscape, rendering the world more "flat" than round. Connectivity and collaboration have opened the global political, economic, and cultural playing field to everyone previously excluded from circles of wealth and power. The future will not resemble the past; to succeed from this point forward, individuals and companies must develop strategies that fit the global realities.[6]

So how do you influence this 24/7 streaming global conversation? By doing what you do best—and what human beings have been doing since God established the twelve tribes of Israel—you reconnect to and mobilize the tribe.

In his groundbreaking book *Tribes*, Seth Godin reconnects us to our human tendency to create tribes. A tribe, says Godin, is a "group of people connected to one another, connected to a leader, and connected to an idea. For millions of years, human beings have been part of one tribe or another. A group needs only two things to be a tribe: a shared interest and a way to communicate."[7] The Internet provides the communication channel for the world. Jesus provides the channel and the leadership to you, the Christ follower. Can you hear your Tribal Leader over the noise?

⊙ let's go there...

It's midday in Galilee. The sun is hot; a blanket of dust covers the weary traveler who comes into town by way of Judea. The townspeople have heard of Him and knew He was coming. Word traveled quickly of miracles, prophecies, and outlandish claims made by this very peculiar, humble carpenter from Nazareth.

"His name is Jesus. Says He's the Messiah," they whisper as He passes. "Son of God He claims...but we all know nothing good comes out of Nazareth." He meets their critical eyes with an expression that lacks both worry and offense. They whisper, unaware that He can hear their hearts. While they are entangled in their quiet chatter, this Tribal Leader hears only their overwhelming need.

The Scripture provides the first lesson in social networking and the importance of community. It points to Jesus as one of history's first influencers to say, "Follow me."

"As Jesus walked beside the Sea of Galilee, he saw Simon and his brother Andrew casting a net into the lake, for they were fishermen. 'Come, follow me,' Jesus said, 'and I will make you fishers of men.' At once they left their nets and followed him."

Mark 1:16–18, NIV

then and now

That day in Galilee, Andrew and Simon dropped their nets and followed Jesus. Since that day, millions have decided to do the same. Jesus promised before He ascended to heaven that He would send His Holy Spirit (the Power Source) to enable His followers to do *greater things* than even He had done (John 14:12). Give yourself a minute and reread that sentence.

Do you *really believe* you can do greater things empowered by the Holy Spirit than even Christ did while He walked the earth? Perhaps if you did—if we all did—things might look differently around us.

Jesus charged His believers to get up and go, to share the truth about Him with the world. He called those believers, and He's calling you, a "light."

"You are the light of the world. A city on a hill cannot be hidden."
Matthew 5:14, NIV

What does light do? It makes things visible and more easily understood. God's light helps others see what they didn't see—or couldn't see—when the lights were out. Your presence as a believer in social networking circles "sheds light on" cultural, social, and political issues, world events, personal struggles, and issues of morality that a global culture all but shrouds.

You will find in this new frontier that influence, persuasion, marketing, vanity, and jockeying for position are the universal currency. Your presence is to be monetized; your message is to be marginalized, to make room for the next, best thing in the Land of Shiny Things.

But your job is to illuminate and celebrate truth in a whole different way.

"Remember, our Message is not about ourselves; we're proclaiming
Jesus Christ, the Master. All we are is messengers, errand runners
from Jesus for you. It started when God said, 'Light up the darkness!'
and our lives filled up with light as we saw and understood God in
the face of Christ, all bright and beautiful."
2 Corinthians 4:5–6, THE MESSAGE

In this passage, Paul tells us that light isn't content to simply shine on itself; it must inform and proclaim a higher message. It sees, understands, shares, and illuminates for others the face of God, that is, Christ.

So in such a time as this—the predetermined time to which you were born—how do you follow Jesus in a Web-based world and lead others to do the same? How do you deliver the only message that matters? How do you make it stick?

⚡ download

- ↻ **Light trumps shiny every time.**

- ↻ **"You are the light of the world" (Matthew 5:14, NIV).**

- ↻ **God planned for you to be born in *this* time.**

- ↻ **Social networks are the communication channels you can travel with Him and for Him.**

- ↻ **The newest mission field is at your fingertips. No passport needed.**

- ↻ **Jesus is still the greatest influencer and community builder of all time.**

- ↻ **Jesus said, "Follow Me."**

- ↻ **The mandate hasn't changed: spread the gospel here, there, and everywhere.**

⚡ upload

Dear Lord,

With one word You spoke the world into being. You spoke light. You spoke man. And You spoke love with Your Son, Jesus. You fashioned me long ago to live and move in this time, and I will man my post with Your authority and Your power. I will speak Your name in the Land of Shiny Things, knowing that only Your Light can interrupt the world's gaze and turn it back to heaven.

All things were created by You, for You, and for Your glory—including the many tools of technology. Help me master those tools to bring Your Kingdom to this earth.

I will go and I will do just as so many have done before me with the tools they were given. Open my mind and open my understanding—for my deepest desire is to follow You and make You known as I log online each day. Amen.

Jesus: the stickiest story ever told

> **@stickyJesus** The world changes, but My message doesn't.

Share

So, are you following Zoë? I've been following her for about a year. She's always eating at great restaurants, reading interesting books, and doing interesting things. Check it out—I even have her status updates and photos feeding to my phone. Pretty cool, huh?

It's conversations like this one, overheard while standing in line at Starbucks, that just a few years ago could have gotten you a restraining order or, at the very least, raised a few eyebrows. But that was then and this is now. "Following" another person online simply means you have access to the person's real-time updates when you join online social networks such as Twitter, MySpace, Facebook, or one of the many other social platforms. They know you are following them, and they may be following you just as closely.

Many of these networks include an ever-growing list of friends, followers, or connections that make up the millions of niche communities thriving online. Such sites have redefined our interpersonal relationships and what it means to be followed or have a big following. Even a word as simple as *friends* has been amended from people you might invite to your wedding to people you wouldn't recognize if you ended up shipwrecked together. Yes, our vernacular has morphed exactly that much.

For millions of people worldwide, social media sites have forever changed how to stay in touch with family, friends, clients, and coworkers. In the landscape of online communities, users share status updates, a

> *Connection is the very core of what makes us human...*

variety of media, blog entries, news, resources, and other personal and professional information.

The degree to which people now use social media tools is jaw-dropping to techies, the press, businesses, and even the college kids who unwittingly designed some of the sites just for fun. But if you were to peel away the layers of any social network and look beyond the graphic interfaces, lingo, widgets, and apps, you'd find beating at the core the universal human need for *relationship*. That we tend to thrive—and survive—in relationship with others is the core of our humanness and a reflection of our Creator.

In his book *The Church of Facebook*, Jesse Rice accurately frames this online migration as the human need for home and writes, "At the root of our human existence is our great need for connection: connection with one another, with our own hearts and minds, and with a loving God who intended intimate connection with us from the beginning. Connection is the very core of what makes us human and the very means by which we express our humanity."[1]

That expression of humanity is streaming online twenty-four hours a day, seven days a week, and it spans the entire planet. In fact, if you were to dip a ladle into any social networking sphere during any time of the day, you would find people from every country, race, and creed reaching out, venting, educating, joking, grieving, making money, spending money, celebrating, polarizing, unifying, inspiring, advising, and even praying. It's a cacophony of human dialogue similar to what you would hear while eavesdropping at a food court or an after-hours business mixer—only it's taking place in a digital environment.

how we got so chatty

It's fun to skip a rock across the history of this cultural phenomenon of social networking. Remember the BBSs (bulletin board systems) of the 1980s as the primitive network messaging boards that allowed users text-only discussions, file sharing, and online games? BBS pioneers (geeks, coders, and gamers) gained momentum throughout the 1980s and into the 1990s when Prodigy, CompuServe, and AOL logged on to the action and stepped up the interface a notch for a monthly or even hourly fee. The social side of those networks stimulated Web sites such as Friendster.com, Classmates.com, and SixDegrees.com, where everyone on the planet was determined to trace his or her social lineage within six people, or connections, of Kevin Bacon. It was a seemingly wild but absolutely probable notion that sparked a quest for faster, deeper, and higher degrees of social connection. These rudimentary social platforms were baby steps toward meeting our need to connect online.

The globalization of the world economy—faster, better communication technology between all countries—encouraged this overall social connectivity. Over the course of thirty years, the social networking phenomenon went from crawling to standing upright with Netscape's browsing capability, which opened the door for Aunt Fran to surf for holiday recipes and cures for her sciatica. Then, as the general public became more reliant on technology, the press outrageously compared Google to God. After all, the talking tech heads of the day reasoned coyly that Google is wireless (everywhere), knows everything, and can answer any question that anyone asks. And if information is power, then Google's ranking is right up there next to God, right?[2]

Just because a technology evolves, there is no guarantee that a demand will support it—at least not to the degree that social media exists today. Remember the Microsoft Zune? The Apple Cube? How about electronic currency? You don't remember the technology failures because, well, they pretty much...failed. Multiple factors can be attributed to why social media hit overdrive in the past several years, including cheaper broadband, a fire to innovate, and the global economy shift. As unprecedented economic, political, and social factors continue to fragment continents, cities, and even homes, words such as *connection, community*, and *relationship* increasingly dominate the conversation.

The evolution of globalization is the progress of ideas. It's the anticipated economic equalizer brought on by relatively inexpensive Internet, browsers, and the fact that no one owns the Internet (yet). All of this has linked us all closer than anyone could have imagined just a few decades ago. This moment in time is the perfect communications storm—a global shift, economically and socially, that has leading thinkers today rendering the world more flat than round and shrinking by the moment.

Connectivity, content, and community—the three Cs—are changing the very shape of the planet. To be heard from this point forward, individuals, companies, organizations, and governments with essential (and profitable) messages to communicate must develop strategies that fit the global realities, or as Bloomberg.com warns: "catch up...or catch you later."[3]

it's sticky

As a follower of Christ, you have an imperative message from Him. The message is as sticky as it gets. It's a message that holds fast; it adheres and clings to the heart of every generation. Sticky content is independent of time, change, and cyberspace. The Apostle Paul, no doubt a thought leader of his day, knew the message was unlike anything else the world had ever known, and he wrote,

> "We carry this precious Message around in
> the unadorned clay pots of our ordinary lives."
> 2 Corinthians 4:7b, THE MESSAGE

Adapting to technology does not mean you change the message to fit the culture. The Word of God stands and does not need to be spiced up or watered down to fit the taste buds of *any* culture or generation. The Word is as alive and active as it was when God spoke it into existence. The only thing that must change is your mind-set about how you must now relate to the culture around you.

Paul got that. When he was with Jews, he kept Jewish laws, customs, and covenants. When he went to the Gentile part of town, he shape-shifted his communication style so as to appeal to the Gentiles. Was he a hypocrite? No. No more than a president who quietly thanks God before a meal in Thailand where Buddha hovers over the dining room and then respectfully joins his host in bowing his head for a Buddhist blessing. If anything, Paul was simply appropriate. Paul *respected* and *adapted* to the culture in which he found himself. Why? Because he was mission-centric; intent that he might "save some." Can you hear Paul thinking? *Hmmmm...should I eat kosher chicken today...or should I watch the guy across from me burn in a pit of sulfur and be separated from God for all eternity? Say, Levi, pass me that chicken!*

> "When I am with those who are weak, I share their weakness,
> for I want to bring the weak to Christ. Yes, I try to find common
> ground with everyone, doing everything I can to save some. I do
> everything to spread the Good News and share in its blessings."
> 1 Corinthians 9:22–23, NLT

Writer and theologian Francis Schaeffer said that "each gen-eration of the church in each setting has the responsibility of com-municating the gospel in understandable terms, considering the language and thought-forms of that setting."[4] It's easy—and even com-forting at times—to grumble about the head-spinning rate of change and the acute pain that comes with it. But as a believer, you have to re-alize that it's time to dig down into the core human *need* creating the demand for connection and respond to the mission field at your fingertips. It's time to care more deeply and communicate better to the world without conforming to it...just like Jesus did.

Connection is about joining and fastening things together. Relationship is about creating a sense of belonging.

The world is wired for 24/7 connection, but you've secured the most coveted connection—Jesus Christ. And while the world oozes multiplicity in its *motives* for relationship building online, be assured that just *one motive* moved God to connect to you in genuine relationship. That motive was love. Love compelled God to send His only Son—the Holy One—to establish relationship with us, the unholy. That same determined love allowed Jesus to suffer on the cross in your place.

"For God so loved the world that he gave his one and only Son,
that whoever believes in him
shall not perish but have eternal life."
John 3:16, NIV

Yes, *love* is an exceedingly odd word to throw into the digital conversa-tion. But you *must*. It's in your Christ-filled DNA that you know and effectively communicate His story (the gospel) to others. Christ's life reflected the value He placed on love as the core of His relationships—even toward those who hated Him. The world came to know Him through love, and it's still through love that today's digital residents will come to know Him (through you).

wired to follow

We are thankful that God designed His plan to be replicated. Jesus came so that you could see and learn how to be just like Him. Because of His ex-ample, you're poised to do what He did.

Jesus maintained a primary connection with the Father, and that connection shaped everything He did. He knew who He was and *whose* He was. That clarity grounded and shaped His perspective. One of the things Jesus' baptism announced was His intention to follow God's will and His recognition that He belonged to God alone. Jesus knew how to live only in a state of obedience.

> *"Then Jesus came from Galilee to John at the Jordan to be baptized by him. And John tried to prevent Him, saying, 'I need to be baptized by You, and are You coming to me?' But Jesus answered and said to him, 'Permit it to be so now, for thus it is fitting for us to fulfill all righteousness.' Then he allowed Him."*
>
> Matthew 3:13–15, NKJV

When Satan tempted Jesus in the desert, Jesus clearly demonstrated *whose* He was (and is). He held tightly to the Word of God and countered every temptation that Satan dished up. He emerged from the wilderness victorious and overcame forty days of intense testing and torment (see Matthew 4). He showed us it's possible to overcome any temptation in our paths.

When communicating in a Web-based world, it's critical to choose the authority of your life *before* you engage in meaningful conversations with others. Be assured, this new mission field is ripe with land mines, some with your very name on them. Remember, for all the lip service the Israelites gave the "Lord" of their lives as they fled the slavery of Egypt, it wasn't long before they were whipping out the golden calf for some home-style worship. They didn't fully realize who or *whose* they were and soon returned to their old ways.

You must maintain a holy, heavenly perspective, just as Jesus did, which is perhaps the most critical mandate for a Christ follower online. This connection to the Father is immensely important, and it is a topic we'll delve into much deeper later.

When Jesus started His ministry, He began to call individuals to "follow" Him.

> *"Jesus, walking by the Sea of Galilee, saw two brothers,*
> *Simon called Peter, and Andrew his brother,*
> *casting a net into the sea; for they were fishermen.*
> *Then He said to them, 'Follow Me, and I will make you fishers of men.'"*
>
> Matthew 4:18–19, NKJV

You will see and hear the expression "follow me" or "I'm following..." a lot in the social networking realm, but to date, no one has yet to offer the return on investment (eternity) that Jesus offered. Once the disciples began following Him, Jesus proved worthy of their trust by being consistently genuine and authentic. Basically, He cared, and it showed as He walked, talked, prayed, ate, and lived out the highs and lows of daily life with His beloved tribe of twelve.

That same trust, built through consistent, real, one-on-one dialogue, is the goal in your online relationships. It will be a steadiness of character, a showing up, and a reaching out with a Jesus brand of sticky compassion that will touch hearts for eternity.

heart over head count

For Jesus it was never about the *head count* of the crowd He addressed; it was about the individual *heart* seeking Him out and eager to respond to Him. Recognize that value grows in the heart of one-on-one relationships, not in the number of people you're connected to online. *Heart* trumps *head count* every time. Be aware that Jesus' approach to relationship isn't the established norm in social networks. Many times people will follow you based on the number of followers, friends, or fans your organization accumulates. Many of these high numbers are valid and based on truly aligned minds; however, many of these numbers were grown by using paid services and aggressive following tactics.

Jesus proved that the stickier your message, the more followers you will have. Once you followed Jesus, you received His value immediately; you understood this was not going to be a regular hike through the hills. Jesus built His community on the Word of God and equipped His tribe to go out and reach the lost, those people living outside of communion with God. He entrusted His tribe to leave a legacy that would reach far into the future and rock lives until the end of time. You are part of that legacy. The core instructions remain:

"As you go, preach, saying, 'The kingdom of heaven is at hand.'
Heal the sick, cleanse the lepers, raise the dead, cast out demons.
Freely you have received, freely give."
Matthew 10:7–8, NKJV

it's a transformation thing

The goal of sharing your faith with another person isn't simply to broadcast *information*; it's to be a channel that aids the Holy Spirit in His work of *transformation*. In reaching out and building disciples online, look to Jesus and His inner circle. Jesus taught and modeled truth, and then He *empowered* the disciples to minister to and warn the lost, heal the sick, raise the dead, cleanse diseases, and drive out demons. Now that's *seriously effective* empowerment!

The best part of this promise is that you have the *same* Leader today. Jesus has drawn you, taught you, refined you, and empowered you to live a holy life set apart from this world. You've been charged by the Father to touch this and the next generation the way He's touched you. In thinking of ministering online, recognize that communities will be the virtual places where God will use you to teach, touch, pray for, and empower others. Sometimes, you may be speaking to nonbelievers; other times, to believers in dire need of God's truth.

Jesus trained His tribe to get moving beyond themselves. He commissioned them to get involved, to revolutionize their communities and their nation with truth. It was a loaded command. Teaching others would require the disciples to embody and exude the very heart, leadership, wisdom, and fortitude that Jesus had. A high calling, no doubt, but the disciples shared a burning passion to *go*. Before ascending to the Father, Jesus gave His beloved tribe their final charge:

> *"Go therefore and make disciples of all the nations, baptizing them*
> *in the name of the Father and of the Son and of the Holy Spirit,*
> *teaching them to observe all things that I have commanded you;*
> *and lo, I am with you always, even to the end of the age."*
> — Matthew 28:19–20, NKJV

After Jesus left for heaven, He fulfilled yet another promise. In the book of Acts, we learn of Pentecost and how a wildfire ignited and spread. Pentecost can be considered the *tipping point* of the Scriptures, the point at which everything changed. The Holy Spirit arrived on cue to complete what was started and to execute the plan for the final finish.

In sociology *tipping points* are defined as "the levels at which the momentum for change becomes unstoppable."[5] It's a concept that undergirds the mysteries of the Web and the power and influence of human connection. Business writer Malcom Gladwell defines a *tipping point* as a sociological term: "the moment of critical mass, the threshold, the boiling point." In his book *The Tipping Point*, Gladwell explains the "mysterious" sociological changes that mark everyday life and end up spreading throughout communities like viruses.[6]

when God hit "send"

The book of Acts explains the mysteries of Pentecost in a similar way, only in Holy Spirit terms. Acts is the account of the beginning and spread of Christianity. It's a book that would not exist without the infusion, guidance, power, and protection of the Holy Spirit. Acts bridges the gap between the Jesus of history (Jesus preaching in the Gospels) and the Jesus of faith (the risen Christ being preached in the Epistles). It's an exciting moment in Christian history that explains exactly how the messenger (you) becomes central to the communication of the message even today as you sit in front of a computer screen:

> *"When the day of Pentecost came, they were all together in one place.*
> *Suddenly a sound like the blowing of a violent wind*
> *came from heaven and filled the whole house where they were sitting.*
> *They saw what seemed to be tongues of fire*
> *that separated and came to rest on each of them.*
> *All of them were filled with the Holy Spirit*
> *and began to speak in other tongues as the Spirit enabled them."*
> *Acts 2:1–4, NIV*

Filled and enabled by the Holy Spirit, Peter took to the streets along with the other anointed disciples; and with astonishing boldness and authority, he preached to the crowds that gathered.

> *"With many other words he warned them;*
> *and he pleaded with them, 'Save yourselves from this corrupt*
> *generation.' Those who accepted his message were baptized,*
> *and about three thousand were added to their number that day."*
> *Acts 2:40–41, NIV*

Simply through hearing, more than three thousand people confessed Christ that day. The disciples didn't form a committee, write a communication plan, or hold a big conference (complete with a worship band) to figure out how to share the most incredible message in the world. They told the crowd who Jesus was and how everyone within earshot could receive forgiveness, salvation, and the same Holy Spirit power that had lit up all of them. They walked onto the dusty streets of Jerusalem with believing hearts and the willingness to be consumed with and led by the Holy Spirit. God could have done this without the disciples. Supernatural is supernatural. He could have let loose a light show on the streets of Jerusalem that day that would have left the masses speechless. But He loved us too much to leave us out of His story and His glory. He was and is a God of relationship, love, and community. He wants to raise His kids by experiential relationship, not dead religion.

The same holds true today. God doesn't *need* you to share your faith to save the world. There's no cape required. He's almighty. He can touch any heart at any moment, anywhere, in any way He chooses. The glory and gift of this holy equation are that He has *called you*. He's called you out of your stunted, insular self and into a limitless and vast relationship with Him. He will do a holy work in you and others each time you recount that story. Now that's a transformational mission worth logging on for.

⟳ download

- ⟲ **God designed you to be connected to Him and to others.**
- ⟲ **People yearn for relationships that stick.**
- ⟲ **Social media tools have created new platforms that connect the world. Are you logged on?**
- ⟲ **The Good News is the stickiest—most lasting—story ever told.**
- ⟲ **Jesus was constantly logged on to the Father's heart.**
- ⟲ **Jesus cared about hearts, not a head count.**
- ⟲ **Because Jesus was *connected* to God, He was able to do all things.**
- ⟲ **You have the privilege of sharing the story that will stick to every generation.**

Dear Lord,

Nothing in this world lasts except Your love. Help me know that love so intimately that I can't keep it to myself. Teach me to speak with Your love, respond with Your hands, and think with Your mind when I am ministering to others and living out my life authentically online. Form the relationships that You desire in my life. I am all Yours. Your truth has stuck to every generation. Thank You for allowing me to be a messenger of that truth. Quicken me, through the power of Your Holy Spirit, to handle this message with confidence, courage, and care in every situation. Help me see the people behind the pictures and tune my heart in to see the "post behind the post." Your message adheres and bonds hearts to You. So, direct me when to speak and when to be silent. I commit to You today that I will bow to the power of Your Holy Spirit; I will decrease as Your Holy Spirit increases in me. I expect, anticipate, and welcome divine appointments online today. Amen.

Jesus: Author of relationships

> **@stickyJesus** I came to show you how.

Share

What can you learn from this carpenter from Nazareth about building relationships with the potential to alter the world? What were His characteristics, habits, and values that could inform and infuse your outreach to others? Let's take a look.

leadership

Jesus influenced the thinking, the behavior, and the development of others. He was a leader. There wasn't a town or a city He entered where hearts and minds did not respond. When He engaged the people in conversation, they listened. When He spoke the language of eternity and performed miracles, lives changed.

> *"They were astonished at His teaching, for He taught them as one having authority, and not as the scribes."*
> *Mark 1:22, NKJV*

Jesus did this because He was God, but also because He invested thirty years preparing for His mission. Jesus was the personification of His message; the challenge for us today is to engage a needful planet effectively for Him. Leadership books repeat the characteristics: leaders go against the grain, take personal risks to achieve a greater goal, and create culture. They're mission-centric. They speak of vision, possibility, and teamwork.

Great leaders are exceptional communicators and standout influencers. Great leaders get personal.

Jesus demonstrated remarkable leadership in His relationships and, in turn, gained phenomenal influence. As His follower, having been given authority through Christ, you too can gain influence in the communities you build in this Web-based mission field.

"But what if I'm not a leader?" you might ask. Perhaps not by the world's standards, but in the eyes of Christ, you are a leader because you have the Leader living in you. Simply put: leadership is in your spiritual genes! Bystanders, naysayers, and benchwarmers are not handed a Great Commission. Every Christ follower is custom made for this mission.

leadership—scott's story

Profile: Scott Williams, husband, father, thought leader, author, LifeChurch.tv pastor, speaker, diversity. Al Gore invented the Internet and I invented the #FistBump on Twitter!

Tools: Twitter, Facebook, blog.

Links: On Twitter follow Scott @ScottWilliams. You can also read his blog at http://www.bigisthenewssmall.com. Stay tuned for Scott's book, *Church Diversity: Moving Beyond the Dream*, coming out in spring 2011.

I think we all have a place as leaders in the world of social media. Our place inevitably reveals itself in areas where our passions lie. As a pastor and blogger, I write about what I'm passionate about, and that turns out to be a unique mix of faith, leadership, diversity, technology, and social media. This mix allows me the opportunity to interact with people from a wide range of interest groups. I have an opportunity to be an ambassador for Christ by living out my faith authentically in the online world.

You really never know how God is going to use your voice online.

One day I logged on to Twitter and shared some thoughts from my morning devotional and simply tweeted, "Jesus loves you!" It didn't take long for one of my followers to respond: "Who the #@$% is Jesus? And why does He love me?" While that may have rocked someone else's world, it got me excited. That one tweet created an opportunity for me to share the good news. That one question led to several other underlying questions, which I was eager to answer.

Just keep it real and be yourself.

We have daily opportunities online to demonstrate real-life examples of what it means to live out our faith. Those opportunities include but are not limited to our tweets, Facebook updates, or blog posts. You really never know who is paying attention to you or what God is going to do through those seemingly unimportant posts. People can and will see Christ through you. Hopefully, that's inevitable in any place you spend a lot of time. Social networks—as in real life—represent a lost and broken world that needs the light of positive, God-loving people. I believe Twitter and social media in general represent some of the greatest mission fields of our time. There are opportunities to connect with many people, who have many needs...it's a place where you can do for "the least of these" as well as follow and support organizations that help the under-served.

It's important to remember that anyone can do this. You don't have to have a special platform, degree, or position at a church. Having a relationship with Jesus is your permission to "go" into all the world and share the good news. "All the world" includes online. If you love cats (although, I don't know why you would), then connect with cat people online. Whatever your interest is, make those connections. God will begin to position you to shine His light in those relationships.

Also, take the pressure off yourself. You don't have to talk about Jesus all the time. In fact, *just keep it real and be yourself.* Your faith isn't a checklist of something you log on "to do" each day. Your relationship with Christ becomes an overflow of who you are and what you do.

When 75 percent of U.S. homes are using social networking (Nielsen), it's no longer an option for Christians to be online in some capacity; it's a responsibility. This is especially true for churches and pastors interested in sharing the gospel. Online is where people are and online is where Christians need to be.

Some advice I can offer from my own experience to anyone wanting to reach out to others online is to remember three things before hitting "Send": Does this honor God? Does this honor my wife and family? Is this something that honors my ministry or place of employment? My eleven-year-old son gets my Facebook posts on his phone, so I keep that in mind. It's always great to add value in the world of social media. As Christ followers, it's important to add *appropriate* value.

For church leaders, the reality is that leading in a church setting and leading in a social network are two different things. Leading in the world of social media can sometimes be more difficult than leading in a traditional leadership role. The social media leader has to lead purely through relational and content equity. There is no positional equity, hierarchical leadership, or formal authority. Followers may not always get the full context around a thought that you are tweeting, pushing, or posting. And, more importantly, it isn't possible to rescind or take anything back. Once you hit "Send," it's out there and it's forever. In order to communicate weighty concepts or ideas, it takes more thought, better communication, and consistently connecting with your community so the gaps aren't so wide. It's a big deal.

I think it's important for pastors to model online outreach for the church. In this realm, not only can a pastor teach others how to interact online and set the bar high, but his congregation will also get to see another, perhaps more personal, dimension of their pastor.

At the same time, don't overthink every step. Be who you are. Find those God moments in everyday life and share them. There are plenty. Many times, I get the most response when I post about random musings while I'm out and about at places like the barbershop.

I think the deeper faith conversations emerge from people consistently seeing me love my family and just being real. I like to say, "Do you! It's a statement, not a question." It's not so much my knowledge or how great I am at explaining a technical concept. It's that overflow thing. That's why social media is such a great medium—by being conversational and responsive, people *feel* more connected to you; it's as if they know you personally, and in many ways, they do. This can lead to people opening up in the moments that really matter.

For me, this approach has opened doors to being a confidant for some high-profile people online both in and out of the church, which always amazes me. I recently had a ministry leader direct-message me based on a sermon he had seen online. He confessed his struggle with feelings of homosexuality. I was able to talk with him, pray for him, and point him to some powerful teaching and resources that could get him through his crisis. All of this happened online. I got to see that person gain God's perspective on the issue. He may not have had the courage to reach out to those around him. So God is making a way online where some people, even leaders in the church, may feel there is no way.

There's never been a day like today for communicating the message of

Jesus to the *whole* world. Knowing that, I try to respond to everyone who desires a response. It may be just a few simple words and sometimes it may be a couple of days later. I believe in connecting with and following most everyone who follows me, which keeps the "social" aspect of social media in tact. To be accessible is what Jesus asked us to do when He told us to "go to the ends of the earth," so that makes us all leaders in the online mission field.

✅ action plan for leading online

- Be willing to state what you believe consistently based on the One you serve.

- Communicate the future, on earth and in heaven, promised to believers.

- Be a bold contender for the faith—speak truth.

- Be accurate in what you communicate. Communicate facts when it comes to news. Don't communicate hearsay or advance unclear information.

- Communicate truth when it comes to Scripture. Make sure your theology is sound and that your paraphrasing doesn't adversely affect the communication of God's truth.

servanthood

Jesus was humble, compassionate, and affected by the struggles, weaknesses, and celebrations in the lives of those around Him. The account of Jesus washing the feet of His disciples gives us a dramatic picture of Jesus' selfless service that would be outshone only by His act on the cross:

> *"When He had washed their feet, taken His garments, and sat down*
> *again, He said to them, 'Do you know what I have done to you?*
> *You call Me Teacher and Lord, and you say well, for so I am.*
> *If I then, your Lord and Teacher, have washed your feet,*
> *you also ought to wash one another's feet. For I have given you an*
> *example, that you should do as I have done to you. Most assuredly, I*
> *say to you, a servant is not greater than his master;*
> *nor is he who is sent greater than he who sent him.*
> *If you know these things, blessed are you if you do them.'"*
> *John 13:12–17, NKJV*

However, His servant heart did not cancel out the godly authority in which He walked. He boldly communicated God's truth and pursued His mission on earth in warrior-like obedience. King Jesus was what so many earthly leaders are not—a humble but mighty servant.

So you don't think you inherited the servant gene when Christ adopted you? Ask for it; receive it; then walk in it. His power in you makes it possible to serve others with confidence and humility. The social media application for believers is simply to *keep it real, just as Christ kept it real.* Rock stars, gurus, and mavens are self-appointed every minute online. Fly under the radar of a culture saturated with self, and plant Kingdom seeds in the lives you touch. Remember, you can't make a difference unless you *are* different.

servanthood—jenni's story

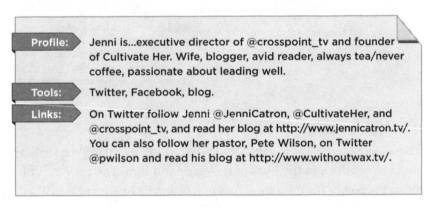

Profile: Jenni is...executive director of @crosspoint_tv and founder of Cultivate Her. Wife, blogger, avid reader, always tea/never coffee, passionate about leading well.

Tools: Twitter, Facebook, blog.

Links: On Twitter follow Jenni @JenniCatron, @CultivateHer, and @crosspoint_tv, and read her blog at http://www.jennicatron.tv/. You can also follow her pastor, Pete Wilson, on Twitter @pwilson and read his blog at http://www.withoutwax.tv/.

Sunday afternoon, May 2, 2010. It's a day that will be etched in my memory forever. I'd never seen so much water in my life, and it just continued to rain... and rain...and rain. I spent nearly two hours trying to get home and there was simply no way. My neighborhood and several of those around it were completely surrounded by water. Penned in by flooded roadways, I found my way to a friend's house and camped out in front of the TV, where anchors had already started to call this "the flood of 2010."

I was paralyzed by the continuous news footage. Soon I began to receive news of not one, not two, but *three* of my staff members whose homes were submerged in water. The tears began to flow when I received a text from one of our staff members that included a picture of the roof of her house...everything else was underwater. I remember literally begging God to "please, make it stop."

The next few hours were a blur. Reality had sunk in, and now it was time for action. Nashville was devastated, and we (Cross Point Church in downtown Nashville) needed to respond. The rest of the evening was committed to putting our mounting worry aside and creating an action plan.

Remember, you can't make a difference unless you are different.

Pete Wilson, Cross Point's lead pastor, and I began brainstorming. We knew that as soon as Monday morning rolled around, we needed to be ready to respond—en masse, to the masses—with the love and hope of Jesus Christ. We had no idea what we could do, but we knew we needed to rally our Cross Point volunteers and just get to it. At 6:00 p.m. on Sunday, Pete and I logged on to our Twitter accounts and began tweeting our plans. Between us, we calculated a combined sixty thousand followers and several thousand Facebook friends—which proved to be a powerful communication channel. We told everyone through these critical platforms to meet at our Bellevue Campus at 10:00 a.m. Monday to help with flood relief.

We really had no idea what to expect. We just kept moving.

Our technology channels continued to be key as we got on the phone with the A Group, our marketing and Web support partner, to create a new front page for our Web site featuring a flood fund to which people could donate. We also added our Twitter feed, stories, pictures, and video to the front page to make it a one-stop news hub for volunteers.

As Monday morning dawned, the devastation was real, but so was the hope. As we pulled up to the Bellevue Campus, we didn't know what to expect. We had put the word out, but who would show up? We had received an overwhelming response of prayers and encouragement from people around the country responding to our tweets. The strength that poured in via our Twitter stream globally was immeasurable. Additionally a team from Jacksonville, Florida—IAmActive.com—responded to say they would be driving through the night to help us develop our response plan. Gratitude can't begin to explain how we felt. Energy and hope filled our steps.

As 10:00 a.m. approached, people began to arrive. They showed up one truck, one car, one minivan at a time with chainsaws, gloves, boats, generators—anything we tweeted that might be needed, they brought it! It was too early to know what the specific needs were, but as we sent teams out, I would look them in the eye and remind them, "You will be hope today. Whether you lift a hand in physical labor or not, your presence will represent hope to people who desperately need it. Serve and love them well!"

For nearly two weeks we sent teams out every day to do flood relief. Some of the tasks were heavy labor; others, more personal and emotionally difficult. Teams sorted people's valuables, cleared out their homes, pulled out drywall and flooring. They prayed with people, they cried with people, they served people...they simply loved people.

Over 2,500 volunteers responded to our call for help through social media channels. A call for help, which began with a few simple 140-character Twitter messages, grew to include a fully interactive Web site, updates on our personal blogs, and frequent e-mail blasts.

In the weeks that followed, the news reports grew fewer and farther between; the mass of devastating personal stories took a backseat to more timely news. However, our social media platforms kept the flood news streaming 24/7. Twitter, Facebook, our Web site, and our blogs kept the needs in front of people. My greatest fear continues to be that the needs of these families will fade away with each passing day as the "out of sight, out of mind" forgotten population.

With limited national news attention and as Nashville herself got back to business as usual, there were still thousands of families who needed to know they were important. Our online platforms helped us keep the awareness of needs alive and rally volunteers as opportunities to serve continued to surface.

Additionally, we received tens of thousands of dollars in donations for flood relief from churches and individuals across the country that only knew of the continued flood needs through our daily Twitter feeds.

I'm convinced it was no accident that our pastor and staff have been active social media geeks for the last several years. I believe that God gave us influence (followers and friends) in this medium "for such a time as this" (Esther 4:14, NIV). The expediency and viral nature of social media allowed us to engage people to serve, as I believe God had called us to serve in this specific moment.

I believe that God gave us influence "for such a time as this."

The Nashville flood of 2010 changed my perspective on just how powerful social media can be. I now tweet and blog with more sensitivity to how I can actively encourage and connect with others. I watch for needs and identify ways that I can personally pray—really pray—for others. I am quick to realize now—more than ever—that when people are desperate enough to ask for prayer, it's because they need it. I look for opportunities to serve and encourage others to serve. I'm reminded that God will use whatever He chooses to accomplish His purpose, and I pray I'll always be receptive to how I can be a part of His plan!

✅ action plan for serving online

- Ask the Holy Spirit to open your heart and mind to needs in your online and off-line communities.

- Ask the Holy Spirit *how* to respond. Ask Him if you should meet with someone in need, make a personal call, organize, donate, or act in some other way.

- Spread the word digitally about community needs, charities, ministries, and crisis relief efforts.

- Share biblically-based resource sites when you see a person in need. Google the need and you will find a link to address that need. Verify the biblical potency of the link.

- Suggest or recommend people who might have specific expertise to your friends and followers.

consistency

When you think about the Trinity, it's easy to miss the incredible significance of Jesus' relationship with God the Father, but that bond is *critical* to grasping the value that Jesus placed on relationship. Jesus focused on the task at hand. He didn't go off on self-serving, random rants (although He easily could have and had every reason to). He was fully God and fully human. But to achieve a nonhuman, higher state of communication, Jesus the Son remained in constant communion with God the Father. For every word, every miracle, and every move, Jesus consistently looked to Father God for *the plan*. Only when commissioned to carry out various parts of that plan did Jesus advance. In the gospel of John, Jesus replied to the question, "Who are you?" by saying:

"Just what I have been claiming all along.
...I have much to say in judgment of you. But he who sent me
is reliable, and what I have heard from him I tell the world."
John 8:25–26, NIV

If you consistently draw near to the Father, you can share your faith in Jesus with confidence. It's not old-school evangelism. It's not a looming responsibility or a requirement that you crank out the four spiritual laws of salvation in the right order. God wants you to go deeper, get more personal, and invest more of *you*—the real you—into someone else. Sharing your story and the many ways God has moved on your behalf is a beautiful and timely *privilege* in this digital realm. Even more so now when wi-fi, widgets, and apps so easily dehumanize very real hearts beating passionately within God's cherished people.

"God has given us the privilege of urging everyone
to come into his favor and be reconciled to him...
This is the wonderful message he has given us to tell others.
We are Christ's ambassadors."
2 Corinthians 5:18–20, TLB

Relationship building online can't be just about what you do, who you know, or how well you can wield your digital chops. Representing the Jesus brand requires so much more. It's more than what you see on a computer screen or in a profile. Often, it's more than what is comfortable. You must see with your heart to share your life and laughter within different communities. Show up, be consistent, and be faithful. Reach into the shared places of sameness, and awaken people to the notion that they may have missed Christ.

consistency—meredith's story

Profile: At the Virtual Abbey...we believe spiritual life transcends boundaries of time and place. Our online community prays the Daily Office via Twitter.

Tools: Twitter, Facebook, blog.

Links: On Twitter follow the Virtual Abbey @Virtual_Abbey, and visit its blog at http://www.thevirtualabbey.com/. Don't forget to follow Meredith Gould on Twitter @meredithgould.

Walk through any neighborhood at twilight and you'll notice the glow of computer monitors radiating from people's windows. They're checking the day's news, scanning through e-mail, shopping online, and catching up with friends through social media. And throughout *Show up, be consistent, and be faithful.* the world, some are deepening their faith and building Christian community by praying the Daily Office with the Virtual Abbey (@Virtual_Abbey) on Twitter.

Although the structure and content of the Daily Office have been established for centuries, members of the Virtual Abbey are exploring ways of adapting them to twenty-first-century life and technology. Behold this bit of wisdom from the Virtual Abbey's mission statement: "We believe spiritual life transcends boundaries of time and place."

This means using different social media platforms (e.g., Twitter, Facebook, or blogs) not only to participate in formal prayer, but also to gather for fellowship afterward in what has become a virtual fellowship hall. For some, these interactions have led to more personal e-mail exchanges and prayer requests. And for some, what started out as a virtual relationship has expanded to include phone conversations and meeting "in real life" (IRL).

The Virtual Abbey, first known as the Urban Abbey, began as a small Benedictine community in Arlington, Virginia, that formed to explore modern monasticism. In 2009, their abbess, Raima Larter (@raimalarter), opened a Twitter account to pray the Daily Office as part of her own Lenten devotions. People began following along and retweeting portions of Raima's morning and evening prayers. A very real, albeit virtual, community quickly emerged and relaunched as the Virtual Abbey when interests and priorities of the Urban Abbey community in Virginia changed.

Since all are welcomed and embraced, the Virtual Abbey is highly inclusive and transdenominational. Recently the Virtual Abbey engaged in a discernment process to select a new abbess. After weeks of praying, the community elected a sociologist, author, and blogger to lead the community. They elected me. I am a convert from Judaism who characterizes myself as Jewish in identity, Christian in faith, and Roman Catholic in religious practice. Honored and humbled, I accepted the assignment. I am a fierce advocate of welcoming all to engage in this revered prayer practice to build Christian community. It's a deep joy to daily witness the difference that corporate, online prayer makes in the lives of those who participate.

At this writing, more than 2,200 individuals and organizations appear as followers on the Virtual Abbey's Twitter account. A slightly different but overlapping community is part of the Virtual Abbey on Facebook. The community seems to grow exponentially each and every month as word gets out about this powerful online prayer resource. A devoted and dedicated core team offers morning prayer (Matins), midday prayer (Sext), and night prayer (Compline), which, because members live in different time zones, sometimes ends up being evening prayer (Vespers).

All tweeters are welcomed and embraced. This online faith community has become a refuge for those who have been disenfranchised by the church as well as a blessing to those who simply cannot get to a building for daily prayer. Plus, social media technology makes it possible for laity, ordained, and vowed religious to join together in prayer—and indeed they do, sometimes visibly in the public stream; sometimes privately, only revealing their presence through direct messages expressing gratitude for the gift of prayerful community.

What draws people to the Virtual Abbey? For some it may be their best option for following St. Paul's suggestions that the early Christian community at Thessalonica get into the habit of praying without ceasing (see 1 Thessalonians 5:17). For others, it's the flexibility and convenience of praying the Daily Office online. But it doesn't seem to take anyone very long to appreciate how much the venerable traditions of praying the Daily Office provide comfort and community online for today's followers of Jesus the Christ. Always and forever, thanks be to God.

✔ action plan for being consistent online

❖ Stay connected to God and be led by the Holy Spirit, consistently adding value to the conversation.

❖ Show up at predictable times so people know when and where to find you. Get back to people promptly.

❖ Present a coherent brand (or impression) that honors Christ (that is, don't post a verse about purity and modesty and then follow it up with a post about going to the Lady Gaga concert).

❖ Be trustworthy in your tone, personality, and style. Don't try to imitate others or retweet or repost content that contradicts you.

❖ Remember whose you are online. Maintain and stay true to the Message. Yes, you can be "in this world," but not of it. People do it every day.

compassion

The accounts of God's unfailing love and compassion for people abound in Scripture. Indescribable love moved God's holy hand to provide a Savior to bridge the gap between life and death for all humankind.

As you daily draw near to God and experience His compassion, your response is to give to others what you've been given and share what you've been shown. It's that simple.

> *"When he saw the crowds, he had compassion on them, because they were harassed and helpless, like sheep without a shepherd."*
> *Matthew 9:36, NIV*

Communication is the most important skill in life, but at the core of great communication, funny as it seems, is *listening*. Building real relationships online requires not that you be understood but that you understand the context of the people who interact with you. If you hear the hearts of others, you'll be ready to lavish them with God-sized compassion. Begin to genuinely build relationship, connect, and care in His strength.

compassion—heather's story

Profile:	Heather Siebens is...where Jesus leads—I follow! Wife of @flyingchristian, Mom 2 Tory, just had 3rd brain surgery—awake—at Mayo Hosp, now fighting bone/muscle disorder.
Tools:	Twitter, Facebook, blog.
Links:	Follow Heather on Twitter @AliveInMe. Read her blog at http://www.heather4christ.com/.

> *"If we are afflicted, it is for your comfort and salvation; and if we are comforted, it is for your comfort, which you experience when you patiently endure the same sufferings that we suffer. Our hope for you is unshaken, for we know that as you share in our sufferings, you will also share in our comfort."*
> *2 Corinthians 1:6–7, ESV*

> *Give to others what you've been given and share what you've been shown.*

Many think when they accept Jesus, everything will be wonderful from that day forward. That isn't the case. God continues to mold us. He watches us as we try to walk in His footsteps and as we stumble. He holds His hand out in every trial, and we have the choice to love Him and take the trial in His strength, or become bitter and turn. The more I learn to grab hold of His hand, the more I understand that His plans are amazing...and I have no problem tweeting those revelations to the world.

I've lived with epilepsy all my life, and I was tired of the thirty-two pills a day to control my seizures. My neurosurgeon suggested, and I agreed to, my *third* brain surgery. Only this time I would be *awake* during the entire surgery.

In the year leading up to the surgery, I plowed into my Bible twice as deeply and shared what God showed me with everyone. I tweeted, posted, and blogged almost daily. The act of reaching out to help others took my mind off me. Some great things began to happen. Relationships grew stronger and God moved in powerful ways online. I felt true love, support, and prayer from my Twitter community. Many of my friends on Twitter were believers, but many were not.

My surgery date drew near and everyone who followed me on Twitter knew it. I could feel the power and the prayers. Looking back, I'm not sure how I would have gotten through without my Twitter friends. I have a great support system in my husband, Christian, my daughter, Tory, and my brother, Troy, but my mother has always had trouble with the surgeries and just couldn't come. On the day before my surgery I was alone for most of the morning in my hospital room.

I'll never forget what happened next. Jamie, one of my Twitter friends, appeared in the doorway of my hospital room. She had traveled quite a distance. We'd never met in person nor had we talked on the phone due to the fact that she was extremely introverted. But on this day, in this circumstance, God moved in Jamie's heart to come. And she did. For four hours, Jamie held my hand, listened to doctors, asked questions, laughed at my macabre humor about the human brain...and just comforted me with her sweet presence. It was an incredible act of love that I'll never forget and one that helped me through the next critical hours of surgery. Jamie and I have been close friends ever since.

My amazing husband kept my Twitter and Facebook communities updated constantly during the surgery as prayers from around the world carried me during the delicate procedure. The surgery was a success. The second I could shake my morphine haze, I asked my nurse for my laptop and began tweeting to my online family. I was in pain but it did not matter. I needed to connect with them, thank them, and praise God with them. It's funny. I felt as if I were related to my Twitter friends by blood, and in a way many of us were—only it was the common blood bond of Christ that made our relationships so deep and meaningful.

People called; some sent gifts. The love and care blew me away. I thought to myself: *It's a busy world. We barely have time to eat, work, and sleep, yet these people were concerned about a stranger getting her head cracked open?* I am still amazed at their commitment, their prayers, and most of all, their love. I'm also in awe of God and the way He comforts His children. In my case, He used Twitter.

My online connections remain strong. I care deeply for people I've met all over the world. I talk to people on Skype. I tweet people in Australia and London. I pray with people from sea to shining sea. I share my love for Jesus through all of my trials with anyone who will listen.

I've learned that we are most alive when we are connected to God and to one another. I've also learned that family—however you define it—is a gift from God and can be a surprising source of strength in the most extraordinary circumstances.

✅ action plan for extending compassion online

❖ Ask the Holy Spirit to lead you in exactly how to respond to others online. Does this situation require you to take an extra, more personal step?

❖ Own and respond to the prayer requests you see. Let someone know when you pray for him or her.

❖ Be empathetic to others' suffering, grief, or fears, even if you can't relate personally. Ask the Holy Spirit to help you.

❖ Keep a prayer journal on hand to keep track of who you are praying for online, their requests and their names. Be sure to follow up. A number of free online prayer journals also exist. Just Google "online prayer journal," and take your pick.

❖ Listen and be willing to go deeper into others' lives; ask them questions to prompt meaningful sharing. Use open-ended questions, the ones that start with "What" or "How." Say to others, "Tell me more."

❖ Let people know when you can personally relate to their storm and how you made it to the other side.

encouragement

Jesus understood people's human struggle to simply survive everyday life: the toil for food and shelter and the battle to overcome the mind traps of anxiety, worry, and despair. Jesus told His followers:

> *"I have told you these things,*
> *so that in me you may have peace.*
> *In this world you will have trouble.*
> *But take heart! I have overcome the world."*
> John 16:33, NIV

No doubt, Jesus liberally handed out hope and always left people feeling better about themselves and their futures (unless you were a Pharisee, then you were usually pretty irked). Everywhere He went, Jesus invited and encouraged people not only to share their anguish but to put it all *on Him.*

> *"Come to me, all you who are weary and burdened,*
> *and I will give you rest.*
> *Take my yoke upon you and learn from me,*
> *for I am gentle and humble in heart,*
> *and you will find rest for your souls."*
> Matthew 11:28–29, NIV

In Luke 12:22–31 (KJV) Jesus told His followers not to worry about their lives in general, the things they would eat or drink or wear. Instead He encouraged them to *seek first* His Kingdom and His righteousness "and all these things shall be added unto you."

People gravitate toward people who are willing to inspire, affirm, and celebrate the highs and lows of life alongside them. Fair-weather, flaky, or superficial "friends" rarely get an invitation to sit and taste the fruit at harvest time. Communicating online is no different.

Go beyond. Reach out. Be that turning point for someone. Go beyond. Reach out. Infuse light and salt into meaningful conversations and the life experiences of others.

encouragement—melinda's story 💬

Profile: ▶ Melinda Ysaguirre is...wife, mom, student. Enjoys God, family, and friends. A woman of faith, not a woman of weeds.

Tools: ▶ Twitter, Facebook.

Links: ▶ On Twitter follow Melinda @JOYFULLTOO, and follow Kim @Kmac4him too.

I've been on Twitter since 2009 as a prayer team member at the Virtual Abbey (@Virtual_Abbey). My prayer life has been enhanced tremendously, and I've formed vibrant, thriving, and loving relationships with fellow Christ followers as we tackle the monumental, global task of spreading the gospel online.

While my main joy online is to serve and encourage others, God continues to pour favor and blessing into my *life* through the people in my communities.

The single most difficult situation I've faced in life was when I lost my mother to cancer in December 2009. I can honestly say that the outpouring of prayers, love, support, and compassion from my online community of family, friends, and fellow believers has had a lasting impact on me. Daily I found myself caught in the merciless jaws of uncertainty, emptiness, and weakness. As I reflect back, one verse remains deeply rooted in my heart. In Paul's letter to the Christians in Rome, most of whom he had never seen, yet cared about deeply, he wrote:

> *"Then, by the will of God, I will be able to come to you with a joyful heart, and we will be an encouragement to each other."*
>
> *Romans 15:32, NLT*

Indeed, this was a pivotal moment in my life. As I prayed fervently for God's comfort and peace, I was deeply encouraged and strengthened by the hearts and prayers of others.

One of the ways God comforted me was through a beautiful, loving, and heaven-bonded friendship with @Kmac4him (Kim McCarthy). Kim offered a beautiful smile that shined from her heart right into mine and a consistently healing word that daily encouraged me and so many others on Twitter. Kim added a profound, genuine voice online that cut across the noise of cyberspace and ministered to real hearts in real need.

Kim was different, and that difference shined brightly online. She and her husband had spent the majority of their lives helping plant ministries. God quickly saw fit to pair our hearts. (Only He can do this amid the *tens of thousands* of faces and voices on Twitter!) We began to discover that even though we lived 633 miles apart, we had both lived thirty-plus years in the same Florida county. We also shared similar values and loved youth ministry. As our hearts grew closer, we began pulling the best from each other.

The more we shared, the more we both felt a strong urgency to meet in person. It wasn't long before my husband, my daughter, and I drove to meet Kim and her family. We shared wonderful stories together during our visit. It was one of the most memorable moments of my life.

Since that time, Kim has traveled to our hometown as well, where we've had the chance to walk the beach, pray, share, and care for one another. We are as much like sisters as we are friends. Through our cyber friendship, God has blessed us with an earthly relationship that reflects the true meaning of unconditional, godly love. Kim wrote to me last year in an e-mail: "God has given us a divine connection—we are forever friends, from here, to there, unto forever."

✪ action plan for bringing encouragement online

❖ Know your stuff. Use e-sword (http://www.e-sword.net/), free bible software available online that's packed with study resources commentaries, dictionaries, and parallel Bible translations.

❖ Apply God's Word. Use BibleGateway.com (http://biblegateway.com/) to do quick topical searches by keyword or verse and find uplifting Scriptures that fit the situation.

❖ Keep an encouragement folder. Collect links to inspiring stories, blogs, e-cards, prayers, videos, and other positive content that could turn someone's day around.

❖ Acknowledge people. You can do this briefly. Just drop a response like: "Way to go," "Congratulations," "That's awesome," "Hang in there," "DM me with the details," or "I'm standing with you."

❖ Publicly congratulate others on successes. You can do this easily on Twitter, on Facebook, or even in a blog post.

❖ Send public or private messages of cheer and comfort to people going through difficult times. If you know they appreciate music or laughter, go to YouTube (http://www.youtube.com/), GodTube (http://www.godtube.com/), or Tangle (http://www.tangle.com/), search for a song or inspiring video, and send them an uplifting link.

inclusiveness

Jesus didn't play favorites. In the dramatic account of the woman at the well, Jesus illustrated His holy rejection of people's ethnic, religious, and cultural division.

Jesus didn't play favorites.

In Samaria, the disdain between Jews and Samaritans was palpable, but Jesus followed God's command to go through Samaria rather than play it safe.

⊕ let's go there...

It's evening in Samaria. The sun is suspended over Israel's horizon of papaya orange. Most Samaritan women came to the well hours earlier to draw their water for the evening meal, socialize, and most likely, score the day's gossip, but not this woman. This one waited until dusk, until evening chores could smoothly reroute "the looks." She walks in silence; each step echoing muted screams of hopeless apology.

As she approaches the well, Jesus catches her off guard. He knows her story. He knows every tattered, stained, and wanton page of it. But that's not where He chooses to take this critical encounter, even though, as God, He could have. Reviving a parched soul with the waters of hope and forgiveness—yes, that was more His style. Nothing gave Him more pleasure than raining down buckets of grace on a misfit dried out by her own shame. She came for water. She left with eternal life. John says that when Jesus' disciples approached the two, the woman abruptly "left her water jar" and ran into town to tell others of the "Messiah" (John 4:28–29, NLT). Minus her water jar, we can only assume she went to bed that night a little thirsty, but it didn't matter. The echoes of remorse ceased. Her sin vanished. And even though she would draw water daily from the town well, she would never thirst again.

psst!...you are human

Clearly, Jesus wouldn't make the A-list in many social networks, and you don't have to feel slighted if you don't make the cut either. Your charge is to stay mission-centric, which will likely be under the radar and making some serious waves for God's Kingdom. The challenge in sharing your faith and making genuine connection with others online is sharing your humanness; it is a confession, sadly, that many Christians won't make in fear of looking imperfect. One look at the cross should cure you of that audacious lie. God so loved the world that He stepped down from a holy throne and became human so that you might touch, see, and absorb His grace and, in turn, *reflect* His glory. So compelled by our imperfection, perfection became human.

So extend your real, flawed, at-odds self to the world.

Your flawed humanness is the most holy thing about you in this earthly moment and the only way the world will get a glimpse of God. So extend your real, flawed, at-odds self to the world on behalf of an impeccable King.

You will likely draw many people from many backgrounds and beliefs to your online communities. Don't be quick to block them. Rather, make room for the spirit of God to move and direct your clicks. Many times, the people God may be calling to Himself wouldn't make the cut for your Saturday barbecue. Meanwhile, God is usually working on another plan...

inclusiveness—marie's story

Profile: Marie Wikle, founder of Spreading Joy Corporation, a nonprofit dedicated to communicating the joy of giving around the world. Have a great desire to give big, but will simply give what I can until that day comes.

Tools: Twitter, Facebook.

Links: Follow Marie on Twitter at @spreadingJOY. Visit her Web site at http://spreading-joy.org/ and follow Spreading Joy Corp. on Facebook. To learn more about #Tworship, go to http://mcprodigal.prodigaleye.org/.

It's 8:00 p.m. EST and the Twitter stream is abuzz with conversations ranging from illegal immigration, to the Apple iPad, to transplanting tulip bulbs. But a group of believers is getting ready to join in a conversation that will transcend the digital hum and take them—together—to a whole different place. A place of worship on Twitter.

It's called Tworship (T + worship), and it's a virtual experience that is building community among Christ followers on Twitter in a whole new way. Tworship uses the hashtag system (#Tworship) to gather people into a Twitter stream. Using a YouTube video of a preselected song, the Tworshippers—from Dallas to Dubai—watch the worship video at the same time (on your mark, get set, go!) and begin writing comments and lyrics in their Twitter streams as the Holy Spirit leads.

"At 8:30 p.m. EST we start rounding up the saints by sending the song selection of the night and encouraging everyone to join us. Tworship has refocused our tweets on the Lord, birthed great testimony, and allowed us to bond as believers online regardless of time zone or location," says Marie Wikle (@spreadingJOY), who leads Tworship alongside Richard Mayhan (@mcProdigal).

Periodically, the group adds a Bible study/group discussion following the two Tworship songs, which they call #TworshipIndoors because they leave the Twitter environment temporarily and go to another Web link (iLinc) for the study. Once there, the group uses webcams, microphones, and chat to continue their worship through study.

Some great revelation comes from those brief interludes of Tworship, adds Marie, who says about three hundred people click on the links, begin to sing, tweet, share, and lift up the Lord together every night. Some people just retweet a Tworship tweet, which is their expression of worship.

God has produced real friendships and real power.

"I'm excited about where social media is going and what we'll do with it," says Marie. "I'm thrilled to be a part of a day and age when Christians can come together from all over the world and just sing 'How Great Is Our God' as one voice. God is so good to us."

Real friendships. Real power. That's been the fruit God has produced in the Tworship community. Marie found out just how real and just how powerful when her teenage daughter, Megan, was struck with a very rare, painful stomach disorder called gastroparesis. For nearly a year Megan couldn't keep food down and suffered through medications that helped her stomach function—marginally.

Marie's heart broke for her daughter. Every Sunday at church, during the pastor's prayer invitation, she faithfully went to the altar to ask for healing. This week would be different. While at church Marie used the Twitter application on her phone to contact @mcProdigal and asked him to rally their online community to pray at the exact time that she, her husband, Steve, and Megan would be going to the altar to pray.

"So the service is almost ending. My heart is racing as I hear back from @mcProdigal via my Twitter stream on my phone that thirty-five people are going to join us in prayer," says Marie. "Believing in what God could do in that moment, we don't wait for the pastor to invite us to the altar—we just go! We ask for healing for Megan's stomach as well as her heart. We want her to be a happy, normal teenager again. We get done, head back to our seats. I get a tweet from @mcProdigal that including Steve and myself forty-seven total people prayed in unison for Megan! What amazing love for a little girl that our online community had not even met. My depth of gratitude to my Twitter prayer family is priceless. Megan very rarely takes the medicine prescribed by the doctors and has gained forty pounds since that day."

> *My depth of gratitude to my Twitter prayer family is priceless.*

✔ action plan for being inclusive online

- ❖ Follow the people following you*—you may be the only light in their world. Engage with someone new every day. Allow new people into your regular communication circles. Welcome them warmly.

- ❖ Invite others to be part of online and off-line events, groups, and causes.

- ❖ Accept an invitation that has been extended to you. Engage.

---

* This applies to "open" networks such as Twitter. However, be discerning on networks such as MySpace and Facebook, where you post more personal information and need to close your circle for security reasons.

↻ download

↻ **Jesus is all about relationship.**

↻ **Jesus led others. You can too.**

↻ **Jesus served others. You can too.**

↻ **Jesus was consistent. You can be too.**

↻ **Jesus was compassionate. You can be too.**

↻ **Jesus encouraged. You can too.**

↻ **Jesus included others. You can too.**

↻ **Jesus' mission was not to inform but to *transform* the world.**

⌂ upload

Dear Lord,

I trust You as the Author of my faith to edit and rearrange the run-on sentence that is me. Replace my words with the succinctness and power that is You. Break my heart for the lost. Help me see beyond the streaming words, faces, and images. Remove the scales from my eyes so that I can see the wreckage behind all the shine. Ignite in me a holy boldness, a deep compassion, and a genuine heart to encourage those You have lovingly crafted. So many people appear to want my time, but that distressing ruse is not from You. You've simply asked me to obey you in the task you've put in front of me, nothing more. The world is not mine to save. Direct me to the ones who need Your love. And help me show them more of You. Amen.

Jesus: Master of buzz

Word of mouth, or buzz, is the hottest, most valued marketing strategy employed by advertisers today. With the explosion of social communities the quest for creating a bigger, better buzz is officially on—especially online.

But if you think about it, buzz officially got its start in the Garden of Eden. That's right. When Eve tasted the forbidden fruit, she recommended that Adam do the same. Had the fruit been unbearably bitter or of no significant value to Eve, she might have tossed it—and its buzz—right over her shoulder without so much as a peep to Adam. But she didn't, and that single recommendation in the garden that day changed the world as we know it. The truism remains: the number one reason people buy or try something is that someone they trust told them to do so. Fast-forward to the twenty-first century, add the million touch points made possible by the Internet, and you've just doused an ordinary buzz with Miracle-Gro.

In his book *Anatomy of Buzz* Emanuel Rosen attributes the word-of-mouth phenomenon to several things, including that we're programmed to do so, we need to connect, we need to make sense of the world, and we wish to reduce risk and uncertainty. "Buzz," says Rosen, "travels most smoothly on channels built on trust."[1]

just a little marketing 101

For context, let's dive into a Marketing 101 lesson. The concepts and ideas here run parallel to communicating your faith online. After all, as a child of

You're in the Kingdom business. God, you're in the Kingdom business. You are called to communicate hope, truth, and life to the world. (No, we are not "selling" Jesus, so pipe down and stay with the story.)

The explosion of communities online has single-handedly taken the pursuit of a compelling buzz to Holy Grail status. Buzz is now a powerful Web-based engine that is running circles around traditional advertising methods.

The rules of the game haven't just changed; it's a whole new game.

Consumers, armed with laptops and an arsenal of social networks, have more power and greater choices than ever before. Not just brand lovers, they are now brand owners. The task of the savvy marketer then is to figure out how to engage people in an authentic, "you first" conversation. And the savvy marketer is doing just that in a number of quite organic, quite remarkable kinds of ways.

The phenomenon of buzz caught the attention of advertisers in the 1970s. Though it's tough to pinpoint the single moment in time that *buzz* was coined, some attribute the creation of the first word-of-mouth marketing model to Abraham George Silverman, a Harvard grad. Silverman conducted focus groups on new pharmaceutical drugs and discovered that physicians who had positive experiences with a drug could essentially sway or influence an entire group of skeptics. In fact, their influence was so strong, ex-prescribers were wooed back to the product.[2]

Creating effective buzz boils down to the quality of a relationship and the precious credibility that comes with trust. In *Trust Agents: Using the Web to Build Influence, Improve Reputation, and Earn Trust*, authors Chris Brogan and Julien Smith describe trust agents as the people who "humanize the Web." They are the digitally savvy people whose modi operandi are transparency, honesty, and genuine relationships. As a result, they wield enough online influence to build up or bring down a business's reputation. Why? Because consistently doing all of these things builds trust. The authors describe today's social networks (like the Facebooks and Twitters of our time) as media "not because they help us communicate, but because they *extend human relationships.*"[3]

This kind of marketing is a far cry from the Saturday morning Ronco commercials where $9.99 would get you...well, anything the fine print said it would, plus shipping. Today's unremitting flow of information is not only fast and inexpensive but also *endorsed* by a group or a fan base, which amps its octane. A study conducted by Opinion Research Corporation International found that users told an average of twelve other people about an online shopping experience. This is the human trust engine that powers word-of-mouth marketing.

Remember the viral buzz generated around *The Blair Witch Project* as far back as 1999? How about the Susan Boyle *Britain's Got Talent* audition video? Don't forget the explosion of the YouTube phenomenon that is now Justin Bieber or the hilarious viral e-mail that allowed the whole world to Elf Itself.

It's mind-blowing when you consider that Facebook hosts more than a million member-generated groups with specific interests. Some of these groups are very creative. Currently, there are more than a dozen groups with a combined fifty thousand fans from all over the world demanding a Starbucks in *their* country. Once a group or fan base is created, marketers have direct access to that pool of potential customers.

Procter & Gamble, Skittles, Coca-Cola, Apple, and Target are using social networks such as Facebook and Twitter to promote new products, build brand loyalty, improve service, and further engage potential customers. Even McDonald's has built a fan group of two million. There are Facebook groups to manage a person's reputation, such as the "Al Gore never claimed he invented the Internet, stupid." Sad to report, the group, created in 2007, has recruited just thirty-two like-minded members in three years. These groups, no matter how random or seemingly irrelevant, represent a marketing intelligence tool that advertisers could only dream of until now.

Let's face it; you live in a culture where people love to talk. People are heavily influenced by the **Four Rs**: *Reviews*, such as Amazon; *Ratings*, such as eBay; *Recommendations*, such as that lovely "like" or "don't like" button popping up everywhere; and *Rants*, such as Yelp.com (and any other place online), where customers can sound off about anything and everything.

You live in a culture where people love to talk.

The **Four Rs** have turned the Web into a 24/7 watercooler hot spot. The power of personal opinion has opened the floodgates for a variety of marketing maneuvers based on word of mouth.

It stands to reason that with so many forms of information pummeling us from all sides, we'd give in and crumble under the weight of it all. But thanks to the rescuing voices of our friends, we can still purchase the right car, see the best movie, and eat the freshest sushi in town.

What's transpiring online is nothing less than a conversation revolution. This is where the true Master of buzz, Jesus, becomes center to this postmodern conversation. We can draw distinct parallels between the way that Jesus communicated and ignited His buzz and the way that contemporary marketers are now discovering ways to do the same.

buzz that sticks

Jesus set the bar high in achieving a buzz that has lasted more than two thousand years. It was a buzz that today's marketers refer to as sticky, or a message that has staying power. The stickier the message, the more longevity it packs, the more attention it gets, the longer people hang out and *listen* to what's being said. Becoming sticky for a marketer is getting harder and harder as the noise level online—caused by increased content and a proliferation of communities—intensifies.

Likely, the word *sticky* has been around since the Tower of Babel came crashing down in a million tiny pieces. Or when one guy got his peanut butter stuck in another guy's chocolate and the idea stuck. There are sticky buns, sticky rice, and sticky notes, and there's that stuff that sticks to the bottom of your shoe.

In the Web world, however, *sticky* is a tech term that refers to Web site traffic. A sticky Web site is a site enjoyed by visitors who will hang out there for a while.[4] Although there are millions of sites, some just do a better job on functionality, entertainment value, design, content, and overall value than others. They are crowd-pullers that have a higher share of sticky.

The stickier an idea, the longer it lives.

Sticky is what all ideas aspire to be. The stickier an idea, the longer it lives. But only one idea is powerful enough to last forever, and that's Jesus.

Wherever Jesus went, the buzz was so sticky that at times it physically forced Him to retreat to higher ground as the crowd flooded in around Him. Another time, His buzz forced Him to preach from a boat because the crowds took over the beach. Attaining such an impactful, far-reaching buzz is a phenomenon that has stymied even the most dazzling communicators.

Can you imagine being in the midst of the Messiah's buzz?

As the midday sun glistened off the Sea of Galilee, Jesus, golden-brown face to the sky, breathed in the constancy of His Father. He climbed to the top of a nearby hill and sat quietly synchronizing His heartbeat to heaven's. He laughed to Himself in amazement as He recounted the flurry of events in the past few weeks. *The time spent fasting in the desert only made Me stronger*, He thought.

Satan in his best scheming could not tempt this mission-minded King to step outside God's plan. And what an awesome plan it was! Jesus recalled every conversation He had with His disciples, every mile they walked. He recalled the children He held and the eagerness in the faces as He looked into the crowds.

Just then His eyes stung with tears...He'd never forget their faces. The adults and the elderly; their eyes mere vacant lots where children once played briefly. Their frames were mangled, their hearts trampled beneath the heartless stampede of life. They came seeking His touch—a holy touch that would transplant spiritual and physical marrow into needful bones. They could actually reach out and touch the Messiah! Just then Jesus' thoughts were jerked back to the hill by the collective hum of an approaching crowd. They poured over the beaches and began to make their way to where He sat. As they came closer, the sound He heard was a strange mix of hope and the stillness that stays behind when hope has been gone a very long time. Were there hundreds? No, He guessed, more like thousands—young, old, wealthy, desolate.

It was becoming a familiar sight as word spread of Jesus' miracles and the audacious claim that He and God were One. They carried the ones who could not walk and guided the ones who were unable to see. They brought those in need and laid them at His feet. He looked with empathy upon His very own and felt all of heaven hold back its tears. *It wasn't supposed to be like this*, He thought sadly as He tenderly lifted the leper's chin. Healing had come to Galilee today and smiled into the eyes of its broken beloved.

secret to the buzz

Jesus was outrageous. Not a freak or a rebel, but a Savior. He turned hearts inside out and rocked the status quo so hard that even stone hearts shattered. One encounter with Jesus and the buzz was on. Everywhere He went Jesus performed powerful, outrageous acts, and the accounts spread like wildfire.

People couldn't wait for Him to arrive. People couldn't wait to be where He was. They heard about the five loaves and two fish. They gasped at the disabled beggar who picked up his mat and walked. They cried out when they heard of Lazarus walking out of the grave. There's not a force in the world that could have pushed back the holy fire of Jesus' buzz.

God is the same yesterday, today, and tomorrow. That means Jesus, through the power of the Holy Spirit, is still fully engaged in the business of holy, outrageous acts. He interrupts, breaks in, lifts up, makes new, and resurrects. He *remains* the chief Miracle Maker and the One who makes the impossible possible.

The world defines a marketing *buzz* as an "oral or written recommendation by a satisfied customer to the prospective customers of a good or service."[5]

Kind of makes you think, doesn't it? If Apple customers can praise and celebrate the newest iPhone and Ben and Jerry's customers can wait in mile-long lines for the unveiling of the newest ice cream flavor, how much more can we—satisfied (and sanctified) customers, saved by Jesus Christ—recommend Him to others within our spheres of influence?

You have the opportunity to give voice to the supernatural acts of God in this day and age. Everyday believers just like you are already stepping out and adding to Jesus' phenomenal buzz.

how far does a tweet reach?

Several different measuring tools exist that determine how far a tweet reaches across cyberspace. Results are influenced by multiple variables, a few being your follower count and the follower counts of those who re-tweet you. Though not science, here are a few examples of *estimated* reach.

Twitter:

Klout.com estimates one tweet by @stickyJesus, a user with approximately 4,000 followers, shared by two mid-level influencers reached a potential of 18,817, while a tweet shared by just one high-level influencer reached more than 84,000 people with one click.

According to TweetReach (http://tweetreach.com/), another measuring tool, @stickyJesus reached a potential of 12,612 people through a combined 50 tweets.

LinkedIn:

According to LinkedIn's Network Stats for a user with 286 connections, the potential for connection (within two degrees, or two people) is 48,100 people and over 3.5 million people within three degrees.

Facebook:

According to Facebook.com, the average Facebook user has 130 friends. While there isn't a tool to calculate Facebook reach (except for business pages), let's assume that of your 130 friends, 10% (13) shared a video or article link with their estimated 130 friends: your single post could potentially reach 1,690 people. That graph only grows, as their friends share with their friends, and so on. If you have more friends, obviously that number climbs.

A complete picture of a person's reach, or influence, is multidimensional when terms like influence assessment, amplification, and algorithms come into play (yes, the influence numbers game is getting more serious by the day). It's not surprising that a number of arguments exist about what constitutes "influence" in the marketing and technical communities today. Suffice to say that if you add up your friends, followers, and RSS blog subscriptions across the Web, then one blog, post, video, sermon link, tweet, or post could easily reach tens of thousands of people in one given day.

Based on the quality of the content, it's buzz, and how well you've actually cultivated genuine community, that number could easily reach into the millions. This equation could go on for pages if we folded in *potential* social networks such as YouTube, Flickr, Ning, and e-mail reach—but you get the picture. Any way you slice it, as a resident of the twenty-first century, you've got the potential to wield some serious digital influence—for Christ.

buzz—worldprayr's story 💬

Profile: For it is by grace you have been saved, through faith—and this not from yourselves, it is the gift of God—not by works, so that no one can boast. Ephesians 2:8-9, NIV.

Tools: Twitter, Facebook.

Links: Follow them on Twitter @worldprayr, go to the World Prayr fan page on Facebook, or visit them on the Web at http://www.worldprayr.org/.

Michelle pulled her car onto the shoulder of the busy freeway. It was raining, and her heart felt every anguishing drop of life hammering down on the roof of her car. Still, she followed the advice of the kind voice on the other end of her cell phone telling her to calm down and pull over. The woman on the phone began to pray for Michelle. With each word, Michelle felt the arms of hope begin to prop up her listless heart. The two had never met in person, but they prayed on the side of the road together that day as a hurried world sped by. *Everything is going to be all right, Michelle thought as she hung up the phone. Everything is going to be all right.*

Michelle had connected to the woman on the phone months earlier when she noticed what looked like a twenty-four-hour prayer conversation taking place on Twitter. What did she have to lose? Her life was breaking into a million pieces, so asking for prayer certainly couldn't hurt. Feeling the shield of anonymity online, Michelle sent her prayer request to @worldprayr. She laid it out. She laid it *all* out: her marriage was in shambles, and her husband physically abused her. She had three kids and had no idea what to do next. Noth-

> *God knows your face. He knows your worth.*

ing surprised her more than getting a message back immediately, assuring her that she was being prayed for by the World Prayr team and its Twitter followers. Then, the person writing her began to pray for her one word at a time—right there!

Today, Michelle is rebuilding her life. The World Prayr team helped her find a women's shelter, a church, and the resources she needed. And, together, they continued to pray.

"It's easy online to feel like a nobody, just a face in the crowd," says Michelle. "But God knows your face. He knows your worth and He will send the right people to help you when you least expect it. World Prayr encouraged me to pray every day and carry on even when all I wanted to do was fall into bed and die."

Michelle is one of thousands who have been touched by the ministry of World Prayr. What was planted in the willing hearts of two men, in 2009, has now grown into a full-fledged ministry. World Prayr consists of an all-volunteer team and looks for guidance and wisdom from a senior team of pastors, people with doctorates, CEOs, and business leaders. The virtual team runs its prayer streams on Facebook and Twitter with team members from countries all over the globe.

"The masks come off online. I think people are afraid to share with people at their churches sometimes because they fear judgment," says Dora, a World Prayr team leader. "They are desperate and believe that prayer is the most powerful thing they can do at the moment. And we are there to listen and serve as intercessors."

World Prayr often takes its relationships built through its streams off-line to e-mails, phone calls, and even face-to-face meetings. Team members field prayer requests dealing with everything: suicide attempts, cancer, affairs, addiction, the deaths of loved ones, parenting, divorce, and job loss. Being in their line of work, they also get to see the upside: the answered prayers, the miracles, the celebrations, the connections and reconnections to the body of Christ.

In an effort to be Christ to others and "put feet on the prayers of others," volunteers spend time researching and connecting people to churches, nonprofits, shelters, rehab facilities, social services, and counselors (wherever they live). They also aggressively build relationships with churches worldwide so that the relationships started online can translate into sound discipleship off-line.

To broaden its reach and impact, World Prayr has expanded its number of volunteer teams. Today there are teams responsible for marketing, offering pastoral support, mentoring, and e-zine publishing. The organization is also partnering with other ministries to provide ongoing channels of discipleship via online webinars. Around the clock, World Prayr can be found passionately responding to the Great Commission, making disciples, and helping all affiliate ministries grow.

God is moving so powerfully through the World Prayr buzz that many of its volunteers are people who once asked for prayer and later joined the team, eager to pray for others. "Our volunteer moderators are amazing," said Dora.

"Many of them have jobs and families and still give their time to get online for hours at a time to listen to, pray for, and connect with needful people all over the world. The whole idea of this is mind-blowing, really."

Just ask Robert, who volunteered at World Prayr when it first began. He recounts: "I was beginning to change my lifestyle little by little as a result of serving with World Prayr...but nothing too drastic. Then things in my personal life fell apart. My wife of twenty-five years passed away and other areas of life began to unravel. The people at World Prayr didn't berate or judge me. They just loved me, prayed for me, and offered counsel that helped me. In a time of terrible pain I should have felt weak but I felt strong. I recommitted my life to Christ and actually led my wife's memorial service. Were it not for World Prayr and God, who knows where I might be."

⟳ download

> ↻ **Buzz got its start in the Garden of Eden when Eve recommended the apple.**
>
> ↻ **People listen to people they trust.**
>
> ↻ **People don't want to be *talked to*; they want to be *engaged with*.**
>
> ↻ **Jesus created the most influential buzz in all of history.**
>
> ↻ **In the first century Jesus did holy, outrageous acts that people had to tell others about.**
>
> ↻ **Jesus still does holy, outrageous acts today.**

⌃ upload

Dear Lord,

You are Jehovah-Nissi, my Banner. Your buzz has captured my heart and set my heart on fire. I am stuck on You—forever. May my life be a living recommendation to others of the new life that I've found in You. I have met with the holy, living, almighty God, and there's no way I'm keeping that to myself. Teach me to war like Joshua, to pour out my worship like Mary, and to dance unashamed like David. Your buzz doesn't need my help; still, it consumes me. All around the globe, the faithful serve You in oppressive or life-threatening circumstances. I thank You that I can reach hearts with a click of a button and an investment of my time. I thank You for calling me forward to speak, to teach, to listen, and to serve others for such an awesome time as this. Amen.

file 05   Jesus: King of content

> **@stickyJesus** My Word won't go into
> the world and return empty.

Today, more than ever, content is king on the Internet. But what exactly is *content*, and why is everyone talking about it?

From a marketing point of view, content is anything that targeted consumers can gulp down with their eyes, ears, and minds that advertisers have carefully crafted to spark a purchasing decision. Don't think traditional ads or commercials. Think fusion. Think articles, white papers, Web copy, video, podcasts, vimeo, music, e-blasts, mobile text, and so on (digital skywriting may be next). If we've learned anything in the past twenty years of the technology boon, it's that nothing is impossible when it comes to integrated ways to share and spread persuasive content.

two billion searches a day

The search for content is the reason you log on to the Internet and why Google racks up more than two billion searches a day.[1] The human race voraciously consumes information (content) morning, noon, and night. Smart marketers accept that traditional means of getting their message heard and that "interruption" marketing are fast becoming archaic ways to communicate and sell ideas. No one is broadcasting. Everyone is engaging. It's no longer survival of the fittest but survival of the chattiest.

The new medium is *conversation*, and the new gold is *content*. Great content makes a Web site, message, or idea sticky. Sticky draws people closer and makes them want to stay.

content fever

If you can imagine the California Gold Rush of 1848, you'll begin to get a visual on what's taking place online from a commerce perspective. Only this time, rather than packing wagons and ships and risking life and limb to gather gold, people now gather knowledge, creativity, originality, personality, and opportunity. They gather these assets into distinct conversation points to upload messages more rapidly, more strategically, and more consistently than their competitors—all in an effort to monetize *you*.

Economically, the California Gold Rush changed culture and even geography, and that's exactly what is happening with the stampede for superior content online. While the Gold Rush occurred just as the U.S. was beginning to feel the growing impact of the Industrial Revolution, similarly, the Content Rush is taking place amid the growing pains of the Internet Revolution.

Thumb through any American history book for a moment. It all began on a cold winter morning in 1848 when James Wilson Marshall, a temperamental carpenter, picked up a few nuggets of something shiny from the American River at the site of a sawmill he was building for John Sutter.[2] The mill was perched along the American River northeast of present-day Sacramento. Following Marshall's discovery of what would turn out to be gold, an economic boom transpired, altering the economic landscape and setting off a succession of events worldwide. By the end of that summer, wood huts and tents dotted the hills above the river and housed the first forty thousand self-appointed miners pursuing the lure of gold and hoping to strike it rich.

Prospectors flocked from around the globe. They sailed, hiked, and rode by horseback and wagon. About $2 billion in gold was harvested from the earth before the picks and panning hushed.

The economic and social upheaval was massive. The entire cultural DNA of the country shifted. Native American cultures that had occupied lands along the paths to California and had been living peacefully for thousands of years were destroyed and lost forever. The Mormon economy in Utah skyrocketed as gold funneled through Mormon-owned banks. Many coastal towns were totally abandoned as eager prospectors left everything behind for gold. The massive influx of fortune seekers from all over the

The economic and social upheaval was massive.

globe Americanized the once Mexican province and assured its inclusion as a state in the union, hence the state of California.

On the day of the discovery, history books concur, Marshall played it close to the vest and was doubtful about his find, thinking the shiny flakes were pyrite, or fool's gold. Marshall revealed the prize from a worn handkerchief, laid out the pieces on a dog-eared encyclopedia, and began to read everything he could about the fragile metal. He then tested the sample in nitric acid from his first aid kit, which confirmed he was holding the real deal.

Both Sutter and Marshall tried to keep the discovery a secret, but just as with any buzz, word leaked out. Soon the buzz of wealth had reached Hawaii, Oregon, provinces of northern Mexico, England, Europe, and even such faraway places as Chile and Peru. It's recorded that some $30,000 to $50,000 in gold was being mined every day by anyone who could physically be present to stake a claim. Lawlessness and sickness became rampant. Greed, ethnic division, and claim jumping by larger, more organized groups of prospectors became the norm.[3]

Lawlessness and sickness became rampant.

By 1849 gold fever had spread worldwide. An estimated ninety thousand people arrived in California that year—about half by land and half by sea. Of these, fifty to sixty thousand were Americans, and the rest came from other countries. Companies rapidly formed in Great Britain, France, and Germany. Mine workers were aggressively recruited from China as the Gold Rush provided an economic salve for bigger woes, such as the potato famine in Ireland; revolutions in France, Germany, and Italy; and the Taiping Rebellion and opium wars in China. The California Gold Rush, which started with primal tools such as pocketknives and gold pans, evolved to hydraulic mining methods to get to the deepest gold under waterbeds. By the end of 1850 the Gold Rush had impacted markets worldwide. Soon, roads, churches, schools, and railroads emerged to support the community. Travel that had taken weeks or months now took only days. A wide range of entrepreneurial activities led thousands of individuals in California and around the world to start new business ventures...not unlike the Internet Revolution of today.

new rules of engagement

As global fluency and power of the Internet spread like wildfire, publishing, broadcasting, music, and print industries, among others, are hanging on to their parcels of economic land for dear life; some are vanishing forever along the way. Media companies are investing unprecedented dollars in social networking education, riding the learning curve, and hustling to redefine themselves or face extinction.

Communication media have forever changed, and businesses are being forced to put much of what they know on a shelf and learn radical new tactics to get their messages heard. Rather than craft clever, enticing slogans or power lines for an ad campaign, marketers are now engaged in a long-term conversation with consumers. Communicators who understand that shift are wholly engaged and making strides. Brands are not just surviving; they're thriving and continuing to break new ground in both practice and profitability. Those who resist and hang on to old media machines out of fear, denial, or pride increasingly find themselves unheard...and even unemployed.

The goal among communicators today is to get their message to the world before faster, savvier, smarter, louder people marginalize them—for good.

People want their share of the shiny stuff.

It stands to reason that Christ followers (and the church) should respond accordingly as the rules of engagement continue to change. Businesses are reluctantly undergoing a daily communication boot camp. And only those who work at online engagement consistently, strategically, and seriously will emerge able to compete. They'll be the ones who lay claim to the mindshare of others. They'll be the ones whose message survives.

Is there one right way to adapt? No. Best practices, applauded models, and commonsense tactics are emerging and being put to the test by the minute. Thought leaders, niche companies, products, and new technologies spring out of any major economic shift. But no one person holds the rulebook. No one technology, app, or platform solves the entire equation. This window of untamed technology has been called the Wild West, and it seems everyone's got a unique, often temperamental bull to tame.

Like prospectors of the Gold Rush, people want their share of the shiny stuff. Only now those nuggets aren't embedded in the earth; they are found in conversations among human beings. The world is in the midst of an irreversible trend altering the economic, social, political, and spiritual landscape, and it is unclear where on the scale of influence the Christ follower will land.

This communication shift applies as much to you as a Christ follower as it does to the banker, the Realtor, or the politician. It's been called the new normal. If you have a message you consider relevant, it is imperative (not suggested) that you use online channels to communicate.

Your best content will come from living your life authentically in front of others and giving God the glory in every step. That's how your story becomes sticky and remains with those who hear it. Many bloggers are finding this out firsthand.

a blogger—dana's story

Profile: Dana Mikels is...a simple girl who is making her way through...8 years a wife to an amazing guy...6 years a mommy to a beautiful girl...3 years a mommy to a perfect boy. All the while learning to navigate through motherhood as a mom of a cancer survivor and a donor.

Tools: Blog, Facebook.

Links: For her blog, go to http://www.dynamicmikelsduo.blogspot.com/.

The children's cancer ward is a very lonely place. The halls go on forever and ever...and you are never certain if the ground you are walking on will hold you up or give way from one moment to the next.

Still, our hearts found one another. Two moms, two sick children, and a shared bond of hope.

My then five-year-old daughter Camryn was in the hospital for her second bone marrow transplant and Erin's* three-month-old daughter, Bethany,* was fighting an infant form of leukemia and heroically undergoing chemotherapy and radiation. A nurse on the ward had a blog, and that's how Erin linked to my blog and where our exchange began. We "talked" through writing blog com-

* Names have been changed.

ments to one another for quite a while without ever meeting face-to-face. We wrote, laughed, shared, and cried...all online.

Then one day Erin and I ran into one another outside her daughter's hospital room. There's rarely a good day in a children's cancer ward, but I'll always remember this as a good day. We shared an instant connection that amazed and strengthened us both. We kept in contact through my blog after our girls were discharged. Bethany had to be readmitted due to a relapse and ended up in Camryn's old room; we talked about that. Erin hoped Camryn's energy and positive vibe would help her baby girl. But that didn't happen. Bethany went to heaven in August 2009. I was so grateful for the opportunity to attend the service and support my new friend.

For parents with sick children, blogging can be their link to the outside world, a way to share medical information and a place to build a small, trusted community. For my husband, Jason, and I, our blog began as a very simple Web page. It was an information channel for family and friends to keep up with Camryn's treatment after she was diagnosed with acute promyelocytic leukemia in 2006 at twenty-one months old. When our nightmare began, frankly, we weren't up to fielding phone calls, e-mails, and questions. Our world had completely collapsed, our daughter had cancer, and now we were left trying to battle through every hour. Our world became very small and consumed by hospital life. We became isolated and withdrawn in so many ways.

The blog shift happened later after Camryn relapsed two years after her bone marrow transplant. We were discouraged beyond belief and left to wonder how to navigate the nightmare yet again.

We needed to unleash heaven's power and get prayer pouring in for our little girl even more than before. We needed people to know Camryn's daily battle and her warrior spirit.

So this time around, we started an open blog. To my surprise, writing my thoughts down and sharing them with the world became very therapeutic and healing for me. I also realized that blogging allowed others to see my Savior in every area of our lives. We did it to tell Camryn's story and the story of the loving God who created her. Blogging is a very powerful part of growing and sharing our faith...and getting through each day.

God moves everywhere, but I know firsthand He

Blogging allowed others to see my Savior in every area of our lives.

moves in the blogosphere. How else do you explain the incredible closeness people feel to one another? You can't. Those bonds are not of this world. I believe such bonds are God's promised comfort in the dark. Through our blog we have connected with a community of people online who have given us incredible hope. We may have started the blog as a way to get information out quickly, but it's become so much more. It's become a way to show others how mightily, and compassionately, God moves inside our suffering. Other families with sick children, families who have lost their children, and the incredible people who know and love us in real life have provided for us a literal web of hope.

Don't try to sugarcoat the realities of who God is and all He is doing.

My advice to anyone sharing his or her faith through blogging is to be real. Be real about who Jesus is to you, be honest about where you are, and be transparent about having no clue where God is taking you because, really, you don't. Don't try to sugarcoat the realities of who God is and all He is doing.

The Web is a big place, so don't be shocked when everyone doesn't see the world the same way you do. Some people's comments have hurt me, but my faith in God is a powerful support, so I've learned to just move on.

I try to be as genuine as possible in my online dialogue. When I share my faith, I'm careful not to be judgmental or to use Christian jargon. The greater goal, especially in a community of hurting or seeking people, is just to love—to love others and their journey and pray that they will notice that your journey, no matter how difficult, is never in vain.

Our journey is not pretty, but it is real. And I can confidently stand before anyone and say, "My Lord is making this beautiful." Camryn is six now. Our family lives each day in a delicate balance between trusting and hoping, believing and living; but we know that somehow the Lord will take Camryn's story and make something beautiful...because that's who He is and what He does.

King of content

When it comes to content, as a Christian, you've got the password to the vault. Not only do you have content; you have *a lot* of content. You have content spanning centuries that has proven to be the most impactful, life-changing content in existence.

about your content gold mine

- There are 1,189 total chapters in the Bible.

- The Bible was written by the Holy Spirit through 40 men over a period of about 1,600 years dating from 1500 B.C. to about 100 years after Christ.

- There are 23,214 verses in the Old Testament and 7,959 verses in the New Testament. This gives a total of 31,173 verses, which is an average of a little more than 26 verses per chapter. (NKJV)

- The Bible devotes some 500 verses to prayer, nearly 500 verses to faith, and more than 2,000 verses to money and possessions.

- There are 1,260 promises from God and 6,468 commands.

- There are 8,674 different Hebrew words, 5,624 different Greek words, and 12,143 different English words in the Bible. (KJV)

- Amazingly, the Bible is actually made up of 773,692 words and would take someone 70 hours to read aloud.

- The number of new Bibles that are sold, given away, or otherwise distributed in the United States is about 170,000 per day.

- About 50 Bibles are sold every minute.

- The Old Testament was originally written in Hebrew and the New Testament was originally written in Greek, but now the Bible is written in 6,000 different languages around the world.

- A Bible housed at the University of Gottingen is written on 2,470 palm leaves.

- The Bible is reportedly the most shoplifted book in the world.[4]

taking down giants

Are you feeling pretty confident in your content? You've been born into an hour in which words, images, stories, and conversation are currency. But God the Creator has been using those connection tools since the beginning of time. His Word has always been His medium, and the world has responded.

Content marketing today is not an event but a process—much like the task of building a quality relationship. It's not an e-mail blast, a blog post, or a Facebook campaign. It's a mixed strategy that uses several social channels. And because it's an evolving medium, the rules of the game continue to morph. It's a world where the rules haven't just changed; they've largely been discarded. So really, the only way to royally mess up your approach is to sit on the sidelines. Today the circle of influence has been opened up to those previously excluded. Small businesses (and individuals) can compete with giants if their content is mighty. That's the power of great content. Smaller companies (or ministries, nonprofits, and churches) are getting acutely competitive (or gaining traction) by having stellar Web sites, powerful databases, e-blasts, blogs, print articles, monthly e-newsletters, videos, podcasts, white papers, webcasts, and SEO, and by maximizing social networks.

As a believer, you have Jesus as your true north. His story and life can easily guide your online relationship or content strategy. His methods were simple and timeless, and many today (whether they realize it or not) are using these methods to make incredible inroads online.

Think about content from Jesus' point of view. Jesus *loved* content. He *knew* content. Why wouldn't He? He was content. In the beginning...there was content and it was God.

"In the beginning was the Word, and the Word was with God, and the Word was God."
John 1:1, NIV

the power that connects

God's content possesses the power. It has carried for centuries what so many marketers are just now discovering as (or admitting to be) gold: that relationship, authenticity, consistency, inclusiveness, compassion, humility, goodness, and love *matter* in a conversation. It's your job to use that Word in your communities to communicate in relevant ways rather than chase people off with archaic, clichéd content.

In a post on Copyblogger.com, guest blogger Mark Silver gives a warm thumbs-up to folding genuine spirituality (not specific to Christianity) into our communications as a way of caring for a client or a consumer: "To be awe-inspired by the presence of the people you are wanting to help, to be humble and not distracted by trying to be something or someone you're not, to feel connected to everything and full of love. And to have it all grounded in deep trust and peacefulness. If your blog posts, tweets, products, content, conversations, and connections reflected that sort of approach, what would that do for your business? Or for that matter, for your life?"[5]

As communication methods radically change, you can breathe easy in the unchanging tenets of your faith. The truths of the Scriptures that define and guide you remain static in the white waters of culture change.

truth to know and share

need	read	what to share
In sorrow	John 14	Trust God w/ your troubles.
When others fail you	Psalm 27	God is our light and salvation.
When you've sinned	Psalm 51	God will blot out ALL sin.
When you worry	Matthew 6:25–34	He's always got you covered.
Before church	Psalm 84	Lovely is His dwelling place.
When you're in danger	Psalm 91	He's my refuge and strength.
When you have the blues	Psalm 34	He delivers me from sadness.
When God feels far away	Psalm 139	He is with me always.
When you're discouraged	Isaiah 40	God comforts His people.
If you desire to be fruitful	Psalm 33	The plan of the Lord is firm.
When you forget your blessings	Psalm 103	His benefits 4 U R boundless.
Jesus' idea of a Christian	Matthew 5	It's ALL a matter of UR heart.
Protection from sin	James 1:19–27	Listen to God, not the world.
Stirring faith	Hebrews 11	By faith all things R possible.
When you're down and out	Romans 8:31–39	God for us—all that matters!
When you lack courage	Joshua 1	Be strong and courageous.
When the world seems too big	Psalm 90	HE was there b/f the world.
When you need assurance	Romans 8:1–30	In Christ = NO condemnation.

need	read	what to share
When you leave home	Psalm 121	He constantly watches over U.
When you feel bitter or critical	1 Corinthians 13	You choose to love.
Paul's idea of Christianity	2 Corinthians 5:15–19	In Christ you R made new.
Paul's rules for getting along	Romans 12	Living sacrifices live love.[6]

↻ download

- ↻ **Conversation is the new medium, and content is the new gold.**

- ↻ **The rush for content is altering the social, spiritual, political, and economic landscape—for good.**

- ↻ **Advertisers communicate diverse, persuasive, subjective messages, but the Christ follower communicates *the* Message.**

- ↻ **There is one content source that covers every human need—the Word of God.**

- ↻ **Be alert to the need. Share the content. You are a Digital Scribe™.**

↻ upload

Dear Lord,

El Elyon, the Most High God, Your Word has dominion over all of creation. It is alive and active. It cannot be spoken without a holy stir kicking up around it. It latches on to hearts; it sticks throughout generations. Your mighty Word is the muscle that holds the universe together; the rhythm of the Love we encounter. It operates in the heavenly realms on my behalf, fires up the morning skies, and extinguishes the sun at Your command. It comforts, heals, and covers Your people around the world. It penetrates to the core of human nature to expose, sift, challenge, and judge the unspoken thoughts and intentions of every heart. A storehouse of life, peace, power, and hope resides in Your Word. Help me speak Your eternal truth with authority. Teach me to trust Your Word with my life. Amen.

Holy Spirit: the Power Source

> **@stickyJesus** Plug in heaven's Power Source and everything changes.

Share

It's kind of eerie, don't you think? While we are infinitely diverse on the inside, somehow we're all starting to look alike on the outside.

We're overscheduled, overconnected, and oversaturated. Minds are gripped, eyes are rapt, and faces share a similar illumination. Our thoughts travel in abbreviated sentences, almost a code to the people standing in front of us, while an enthusiastic digital banter takes place south of our fingertips. With Bruce Lee agility we can text, talk, walk, *and* snatch a fly in midair with chopsticks...without even looking up to make eye contact.

Every generation forms its own collective, homogeneous brand, and today's generation has solidified its niche. The 1950s had beehives and conservatism. The 1960s swung the opposite direction with long hair and freedom. The 1980s had fuchsia hair and pop culture. Today's generation clicks past hair altogether (who cares?) and has become the thumb culture[1]— dominating keypads, cell phones, and joysticks; it's the era captivated by hyperconnectivity.

don't log on without Him

So how do you catch the eye and influence the heart of a world steeped in digital overdrive? How do you honor the message you carry and at the same time genuinely adapt to impact your mission field?

By remembering—at all times—*who* you are and *whose* you are. In order to do that, you must remain in communion with and rely on the Holy

Spirit at all times. It's not a Sunday thing. It's not a Bible study or a life group thing. It's a one-on-one, intimate, powerful, unbreakable Creator-created connection.

But there's a problem. Not all of us have read the user manual. While many people have the hardware (which we'll call biblical knowledge), few people download the software (which we'll call the Holy Spirit) that came inside their package of salvation. So, their bandwidth, power, and capabilities are running at half-speed.

Renowned theologian A. W. Tozer said of this chosen condition: "If we will let Him, Christ will do in us and through us that which He did in and through the committed believers after Pentecost. The potential is ours. Do we dare believe that the faithful Christian believers may yet experience a great new wave of spiritual power?"[2]

Without reliance on the Holy Spirit, there will be no—or minimal—fruit of the Spirit. There will be no revival in the land.

"The fruit of the Spirit is love, joy, peace, patience, kindness, goodness, faithfulness, gentleness and self-control."
Galatians 5:22–23, NIV

The Holy Spirit is the global positioning system (GPS) you need to operate online. He is the Power Source that will keep your heart fixed and ministry fruitful. He makes your life and God's Word sticky to the rest of the world. So don't log on without Him.

The only catch? You have to plug in the Source if you want the juice. A lamp on a desk won't help you see unless you plug the cord into the electrical socket in the wall.

got gaps?

As the Author of relationship and the Master of buzz, Jesus didn't just call His followers; He equipped them. His followers were passionate, resilient, intuitive communicators of the gospel (most of the time). But there were gaps in their résumés. Big gaps. Where would they begin? Where would they go? What would they tell people? How would they mobilize? How would they influence such vastly different communities and cultures? What would they say in awkward situations? How would they respond to criticism?

The mission sounded impossible to them. And really, it was. Jesus knew that. Think about it. If Jesus had left His followers empty-handed when He went back to Heaven, they would have had to rely on their own genius. They'd do what any self-reliant preacher does: rent a used van, go on tour, preach a few dozen inspiring sermons, and motivate a few hundred lost souls—for a little while. Minus the Holy Spirit following Jesus' resurrection, the world would have been left to rationalize Jesus' freakish miracles. They'd scratch their heads, offer up a few shaky explanations, and keep their eyes peeled for the *real* Messiah. Yes, by the disciples' limited thinking, the mission ahead was impossible.

But where man's greatest critical thinking ends, the Holy Spirit is just getting started.

In John's gospel, chapters 14–16, Jesus made it clear to the disciples that things were about to change. He was going home, and they would soon be on their own to carry His message to the world. This is not the time to lose your heads, He told them. Instead it's time to light this place up like the Fourth of July—to plug in the Holy Spirit—and take this ministry and message to the next level and *do even greater works*!

Jesus was essentially handing His followers the keys to the Ferrari and saying, "Here you go. It's yours." He knew the challenges coming their way. There would be too many people with too many needs, too much of the hard stuff tangled into each day, and never enough hours to handle it all. Do these conditions sound familiar?

The Holy Spirit is your *always*. That reality doesn't change when you log online with a profile and screen name. The online mission field is atypical, but so too is the Holy Spirit. He bobs and weaves into the context of any culture, distills the complicated, and bridges the gaps in our spiritual résumés.

*"The Spirit searches all things, even the deep things of God.
For who among men knows the thoughts of a man except the man's
spirit within him? In the same way no one knows the thoughts
of God except the Spirit of God."*
1 Corinthians 2:10–11, NIV

*"The Counselor, the Holy Spirit, whom the Father will send in my name, will
teach you all things and will remind you of everything I have said to you."*
John 14:26, NIV

A heart alert and handed over to the Holy Spirit can change exactly everything.

Can the Holy Spirit help "nontechnical" (air quotes encouraged) people navigate the channels of social media? You bet! He equips you to touch others, even if you haven't got a clue about what Ning, Bing, Tumblr, or Twitter is. It's safe to say He has moved bigger mountains.

He's doing all of this and more, right now online. He's turning introverts into dynamic Kingdom connectors online. He's rising up teens to be texting evangelists. He's teaching grandmas to become technically savvy Twitter pros. He has turned thousands of "nonwriters" into influential Kingdom bloggers and nuns into digital prayer warriors who minister to thousands of people a day online.

power up

The Holy Spirit is your first, last, and most important connection. Everyone and everything else in the Land of Shiny Things must stand down until the Holy Spirit gives you the green light to power up. Open your heart and let Him fill you, and the cascade of light will be obvious throughout your day. Start with prayer, read the Word, and communicate first with God about His agenda. Ask the Holy Spirit to help you grow and deepen your circle of influence online, and direct you to the right people, tools, and topics. Make it a habit of daily *asking* the Spirit to help you. Then listen. Really listen.

Here's a great passage of Scripture to meditate on early in your day before you go online. Tape it to your computer, or put it on your desktop as a screensaver:

> *"Finally, brothers, whatever is true, whatever is noble, whatever is right, whatever is pure, whatever is lovely, whatever is admirable— if anything is excellent or praiseworthy—think about such things."*
> *Philippians 4:8, NIV*

A heart alert and handed over to the Holy Spirit can change exactly *everything*.

In *Forgotten God*, author and pastor Francis Chan challenges believers to take thirty seconds to dwell on the fact that God is actually living *in* them: "Astonished? This is not a distant, loose connection. This is the Spirit of God choosing you and me to be His dwelling place. And because of this reality, stress and tiredness and impatience don't have to define my day."[3]

It's impossible to reach the sacred places of people's hearts if your own heart is inaccessible to the spirit of God. Meditating on the holy things of God will give you a heart that can withstand and enlighten any situation headed your way. You will be more alert to opportunities for sharing. Online, you will be able to read between the lines of conversations, see the tweet *behind* the tweet and the post *behind* the post. You will be able to preach, teach, and even heal like the disciples if the Holy Spirit so moves.

> *"I tell you the truth, anyone who has faith in me will do what I have been doing. He will do even greater things than these, because I am going to the Father. And I will do whatever you ask in my name, so that the Son may bring glory to the Father. You may ask me for anything in my name, and I will do it."*
> John 14:12–14, NIV

wise engagement

One of the first steps to engaging online is organizing your thoughts so you can add value to a conversation. Tangled thoughts can lead to misunderstandings and confusion, and they may hurt an online relationship in the same way it's easy to put your foot in your mouth anywhere else. Ask the Holy Spirit to order your mind, manage your time, and speak a fresh message through you in e-mails, status updates, tweets, or blogs.

learn the culture

If you were headed to Tanzania to do missions work, you'd be required to spend at least a year studying the language, the culture, and the traditions of the people there. Missionaries preparing to go into foreign lands face very real issues of diversity, cross-cultural differences, culture shock, and assimilation. The same can be said about Christ followers serious about sharing their faith online. The Internet (social networks in particular) has a culture all its own. That culture has its own language, protocols, systems, hierarchies, subcultures, and mores. The first step in learning the culture of a specific online community is just to buzz around.

Ask yourself: How do the people interact with one another? Is there a casual, fun, or more formal dialogue taking place? Who seems to be the leader? Who are the influencers? What's the ratio of personal versus professional information being shared? Are there subcommunities, online gatherings, or real-time gatherings outside this space? What can I add to this conversation to be of service?

Take notes. Have fun. Grow your knowledge daily. There's no rush to know it all or to know it all right now. The good news is that when you're gearing up for the online mission field, you can skip the Swahili classes altogether! You'll find great company within the online learning curve, and soon you'll be able to coach (disciple) someone else on the cultural nuances of this new land.

listen

Listening is one of the deepest acts of love you can extend to another person.

Few people really listen anymore. In fact, it's becoming a lost part of our cultural heritage, like playing board games or writing letters.

Becoming a great listener can be problematic because it requires you to give up the sound of your own voice. Or in the online scenario, it's the sight of your own brilliant thoughts in print. Listening requires an "others first" mentality.

> *Listening is one of the deepest acts of love you can extend to another person.*

Until you give the Holy Spirit full custody of your tongue (and your eager fingers) and start to really listen, your relationships will suffer. Great ministry is led by great listeners. How can you share truth in the context of another person's unique life experiences if you don't stop talking and really, really, really listen? You can't.

be tolerant

Being online isn't seizing a one-way pulpit, teaching a theology lesson, or having an opportunity to expose the kinks in someone else's armor. Being online is being in a conversation with *real people* who have *real needs* and really, really, really diverse opinions. Think about logging online much the way you think about walking into a business or social mixer, and act accordingly. In time, if you frequent that community enough, that mixer may evolve into more of a backyard barbecue. If you are fortunate, you may even be invited to the next Bat Mitzvah. Different levels of conversation take place in different environments, so keep the conversation appropriate.

Exercise extra discernment. Sharing your faith online is not like taking a cliff dive where you fire off a debate over the tenets of the Westminster Catechism or dissect modern ecumenicalism. (Yes, that's *exactly* why...) It's also not the place to plow into complex social debates or politician bashing. Blogs and Web sites that serve those niche audiences have also become powerful ministry tools that provide the exception here.

seek common ground

Discovering sameness is the secret sauce to connecting with someone else online. This happens when you get intentional about your mind-set. Before you log on, you must shed any defensiveness, assumptions, or bias you may have toward a person, group, or organization.

Discovering sameness is the secret sauce to connecting.

If you are serious about real connections with real people, you'll spend some time on this. Open your heart and mind to the Holy Spirit. Ask Him to search you out and shine His light on hidden prejudices and sin. Everyone has them. Resolve to begin with a clean slate, just as you'd hope others would when approaching you for the first time (regardless of what they might think about Jesus freaks!).

Think of yourself as a groundskeeper. It's your job to seek out, care for, and nurture the common ground within your community. Enter each conversation *expecting* to discover the things that matter most to others. Who knows, you may be one click away from meeting a rodeo clown with a law degree or a gator wrangler who is also a quilting buff. You just never know what adventures and learning opportunities await. Notice people's hobbies, favorite sports teams, or professions. After a week or two online, you might be surprised—and charged—to discover how very much very different people can have in common.

be present

The spirit of God has the ability to multiply human effort. In the book of Acts thousands of people professed Christ after hearing the Spirit-filled sermons of a few ignited men. In the same way, the Spirit will multiply your reach to hundreds, perhaps thousands, while at the same time help you be mindfully present to those in your immediate path. Active listening will do wonders for any relationship.

You've been there, standing in front of another person who is smiling and nodding as you talk to her, but whose mind is parasailing somewhere off the coast of Maui. Conversation with a head nodder is *not* conversation. The same disengagement happens online.

Take your cue from the One who knows better than anyone how to be present. Those who met Jesus knew instantly that His heart, mind, and spirit were engaged. His eyes were landlocked on the hearts in front of Him. He was a fusion of God and man, and His whole aura was charged with a holy, magnificent *presence*. He was electrifying.

In the gospel of Mark we get a glimpse of what it looks like to be present. A woman, hemorrhaging for twelve years, desperately needed someone to be present in her suffering, and Jesus was that Someone.

ⓕ let's go there...

It had been years. And each doctor told her the same thing: "We can't help you. There is no cure." She left. Inebriated with anguish, confused with despair, she stumbled through the streets. Exhausted tears dried and caked around her soul until all hope was cut off. It's a condition that numbs the body and then the mind until it eventually reaches the heart. She wondered: *Will they find me on the street tomorrow as if I'd been bludgeoned to death? They'd be right. They will tag my toe "no cure" and lay me in the ground where the hemorrhaging will continue...forever.*

Just as she replayed this one-woman act in her head, she overheard some townspeople talking about a man, a healer, who had come by boat across the Sea of Galilee. Their excitement escalated. When they recounted His words, her wilted heart began to rouse. When they spoke of His miracles, it sat upright. The delicate woman dropped to her knees, breaking beneath the weight of maybe. *Belief is such a slippery slope*, she reasoned. *And I am dog-tired.*

Just then, she caught a glimpse of Him. He was coming toward her. Yes, He was coming! A surprising surge of faith flooded her heart, making her feel like a child again. Yes, He was Jehovah-

Rapha, her Healer. The wonderful certainty wrapped around her. The bleeding daughter of an able King reached out with her last bit of everything. *If I could just touch...You...just a touch...please...almost...I must...touch You...It's me, Daddy. Stop...please...I need You...*

She managed to touch a small corner of His robe just seconds before the crowd carried Him away like a leaf on a river.

He sensed power leave Him. He stopped. He was present. "Who touched My clothes?" He asked. His eyes scanned the faces and rested on His daughter, now kneeling at His feet, fully healed. Trembling, she emptied every drop of need then and there. His presence swallowed her whole. And the chains of a "no cure" life broke in a million little pieces and vanished into the dusty streets of Galilee.

keep it simple and powerful

In the online world, less is more. No one has the time or desire to sit and read big blocks of copy. Perhaps that's why microblogging sites such as Twitter have skyrocketed.

People want to consume their content in bite-sized pieces, and they don't have time to dish up much more in return. Ask the Holy Spirit to help you keep your message simple, brief, and powerful in any forum, be it a blog post, a status update, a video, a comment, or a review. Even though you may be in a room alone, you are interacting with—or at least exposing your message to—hundreds, if not thousands, of very real people. The goal is to balance input (what you say), interaction (what you hear), value (what you add), and follow-up (what you give).

be an original

Ask the Spirit to help you find your personal *brand balance* online. Try to keep your posts, updates, profile information, and tweets positive in tone while remaining true to your unique voice. Does "positive" mean that all believers have to blast rays of sunshine or crank out Norman Vincent Peale quotes all day? Not quite. It means that our lips need to match our lives, so staying positive and hopeful—in any situation—is doable for the person attempting to follow Christ.

Judy Garland said it well: "Always be a first-rate version of yourself, instead of a second-rate version of somebody else." That warning needs to go on the back of the perfect little box so many Christians strive to fit themselves into.

Don't buy the lie. Show your freckles. Share your pain. "Fearfully and wonderfully made" (Psalm 139:14, NIV) means just that. In an online culture that aspires to cultivate real connection, showing up in anyone else's skin but your own would be futile...not to mention fraudulent. So trust the person of Christ and keep it real.

keep your words in check

Let's face it. The more you talk, the greater your chances, statistically, of saying the wrong thing. The tongue can be an unruly, vexing appendage at times; it can be prone to mock, judge, or join in all the reindeer games online.

It's only natural when sharing content online that the lines get blurred from time to time. You might repost, forward, or share a joke or story with an inappropriate edge to it because it is clever, artistic, executed well, or fresh in your inbox as the viral flavor of the day and you want to feel included in the fun.

It's easy to rationalize anything that is funny, clever, or cute; however, when "funny" is held up next to the person and heart of Christ, it may be offensive, unsubstantiated, or at worst, racist. Be very, very careful. Submit to the authority of the Holy Spirit in all you say and do online. Never let your guard down, and make sure your posts, tweets, or updates reflect and honor God. If you are reposting a link, be sure to *read the entire post* before you recommend it to a friend. Many times bloggers will include an inappropriate reference, word, or photo in the very paragraph you skimmed past. What you share with others—even if you did not author it—is a reflection of you and the One you follow.

Be a connector, not an obstacle, to eternity.

Be a connector, not an obstacle, to eternity. When in doubt about content, ask yourself this: Is this joke, political statement, funny e-mail, or video worth keeping another person from knowing the saving grace of Jesus Christ? Or am I serving as a channel of God's truth by sending this e-mail?

respond well

The online world is a virtual petri dish where misunderstandings, gossip, and factual errors breed exponentially. The responsibility to think before you tweet, update, post, share, or blog is enormous (think enormous *times ten*). Just as you are to manage your heart, mind, and words off-line, the same principle stands when you are online—in fact, even more since content can go viral in a matter of seconds. It's easy to get carried away and think you are tapping a keyboard alone at home, but your words, heart, and thoughts are exposed to a room full of people at all times when you are logged on to a social network.

Careers can vanish, friendships can be destroyed, and stereotypes can be reinforced by your choice of words. Emotions make it hard to separate facts from feelings, so it's always better to *respond* (especially to criticism) with facts rather than to *react* with emotion. If you are emotionally charged over an issue or an online comment, give yourself a time-out for a few hours or even a few days before logging back on or responding. The Holy Spirit will give you the discernment and self-discipline you need.

it's about His character

Only the Holy Spirit can save people from themselves. Conducting yourself in a manner worthy to follow Christ online and off-line is a daily practice of humility and surrender. Through the Holy Spirit, bring an awakened heart to your online conversations.

People will notice that you notice.

What does an awakened heart look like online?

People will notice that you *notice*. You are quick to gravitate to what matters, and you catch details of a conversation that others might miss. An awakened heart responds promptly when someone is reaching out, even on the days it feels swamped. It acknowledges and encourages others and empathizes with their sufferings. An awakened heart is blind to status, title, celebrity, or nationality. An awakened heart breaks for the lost.

You can't give what you don't have. If your heart is callous, seek out Jehovah-Rapha, your Healer—the same one who healed the bleeding woman in the street that day. Touch His robe as He passes by, and believe that only He can resuscitate your heart. Regardless of what the rest of the world values, talks about, listens to, or views, design your life after the awakened, present heart of Christ.

Psalm 139 says that you express God's creation uniquely, that you are "wonderfully" made. God designed your spirit with immeasurable creativity and distinct purpose. Your "wonderful" is just that unless it contradicts the character of God or confuses the intent of His Word. Until you step into heaven, you will be in the refining process. That's OK. The Refiner loves you. He will allow situations that put a spotlight on the yet unsurrendered places of your heart that may trip others up. God commands (does not ask) His followers to be of "one mind" when communicating the life-saving truths of the gospel. He expects us to reflect the values, behaviors, and holiness of Christ online (and off-line) at all times.

"Only let your manner of life be worthy of the gospel of Christ,
so that whether I come and see you or am absent,
I may hear of you that you are standing firm in one spirit,
with one mind striving side by side for the faith of the gospel."
Philippians 1:27, ESV

"If food causes my brother to stumble, I will never eat meat again, so
that I will not cause my brother to stumble."
1 Corinthians 8:13, NASB

To understand the character of God, study His Word and align your words and actions with *His attributes*, shedding the "stuff" in you that runs against the grain of His holiness. Adapt His character and His worldview over the more tangible values and views of the world. Remind yourself daily of who God is and what He expects you to be and become.

who is God?

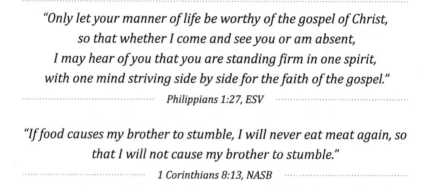

- ❖ **God is love** *(1 John 4:8)*.
- ❖ **God is holy** *(Psalm 99:3)*.
- ❖ **God is good** *(Psalm 136:1)*.
- ❖ **God is truthful** *(Numbers 23:19)*.
- ❖ **God is faithful** *(1 Thessalonians 5:24)*.
- ❖ **God is righteous** *(Psalm 71:19)*.
- ❖ **God is compassionate** *(Lamentations 3:22–23)*.
- ❖ **God is wise** *(Romans 16:27)*.
- ❖ **God is forgiving and kind** *(1 John 1:9)*.

↻ download

↻ **Your true power source isn't Wi-Fi, it's the Holy Spirit. Don't log on without Him.**

↻ **You've got gaps. The Holy Spirit will lead you and complete you.**

↻ **Your time off-line with God will amplify your online reach.**

↻ **The strength of a relationship is directly proportional to how present you are in it.**

↻ **Ask the Holy Spirit to awaken, speak to, and claim your heart.**

↻ **Reflect who God is in all you do.**

⌂ upload

Dear Lord,

You are so fantastically kind to me. You sent Your Son because You loved me and said there's nothing good You would withhold from me. I believe that. My one desire is to be filled with Your Holy Spirit—so do Your supernatural, holy work, Lord, and come quickly. I need Your spirit to guide me, teach me, search me, and take up residence in every secret place of my heart. Holy Spirit, You are welcome here. Own my thoughts, reign over my words. Quicken my heart to respond to the needs of those around me. Tear down the me that offends You. Obliterate my pride, selfishness, judgment, and indifference. Build in me a holy fortress that will withstand any attack. I want to love who You love. Have Your way with me as I surrender joyfully to the authority and power of Your Holy Spirit. Amen.

Christ followers: the game changers

@**stickyJesus** I've called you to change the game for My glory.

Throughout history, game changers have stepped forward in the faith to affect the way people communicate God's truth in the culture in which they live.

Rewind two thousand years and look at the Apostle Paul, the ultimate game changer. Before his conversion, Paul (formerly Saul of Tarsus) was a feared Roman Pharisee, widely known for persecuting Christians. But that all changed when Paul had a radical encounter with the spirit of Jesus Christ while walking on the road to a city called Damascus. That day, Saul became Paul, one of the most significant communicators of Christianity. That day, the game changed.

Paul revolutionized the world in which he lived. He didn't use warfare or weapons; he used *words*. He influenced popular culture one word, one letter, one sermon, one prayer, and one community at a time. *He did something* with the message he carried. He mobilized others.

When the spirit of Jesus spoke to Paul on the road that day, He laid it out for him:

"Now get up and stand on your feet. I have appeared to you to appoint you as a servant and as a witness of what you have seen of me and what I will show you. I will rescue you from your own people and from the Gentiles. I am sending you to them to open their eyes and turn them from darkness to light, and from the power of Satan to God, so that they may receive forgiveness of sins and a place among those who are sanctified by faith in me."

Acts 26:16–18, NIV

The Spirit said it to Paul in the first century, and He's saying it to every one of us in the twenty-first century. Acts 26:16–18 remains our rally call today. Let's break it down this way:

our rally cry

Get up on your feet *(move)*.
You've been appointed *(chosen)*.
Share what you've been shown *(communicate)*.
I will rescue you from humankind *(courage)*.
Open their eyes *(influence)*.
I am sending you *(authority)*.
It is a message bigger than you *(salvation)*.

Paul mobilized the message of salvation through Christ. He carried it and shared it, and it changed everything for those who heard it. Paul became the leading missionary to the Gentiles and penned more letters—thirteen of the twenty-seven New Testament letters—than any other writer.

Just as Paul's letters and sermons became the communication channels that God used to change the culture, the Internet is our channel today that could change the game—eternally—for countless people.

Do we *really* get that?

Marketers get that. Universities get that. Political parties get that—now.

critical moments

Let's revisit an important moment in recent history. In 2008 a little-known senator from Illinois defeated well-known Hillary Clinton to win the Democratic U.S. presidential nomination. He went on to defeat the Republican nominee and now enjoys his morning coffee in the Rose Garden.

President Barack Obama occupies the most powerful elected office on the planet. And he used social networks, in large part, to get there. The issue of social media is nonpartisan. No one owns it or controls it. Any way you write it, pitch it, or lobby it: Obama had a visionary social media advisory team who rolled up their sleeves and methodically reached into, and influenced, the mindshare of America.

Using social media, Obama's message of "change" pulled up a chair at family dinner tables, in college dorm rooms, at high school pep rallies, in the boardrooms of nonprofits, in the sanctuaries of churches, in special interest groups, and at Rotary Club lunches across America. For the first time in history a presidential candidate created a virtual, digital community using blogs, texts, podcasts, Facebook, MySpace, Twitter, and a dozen other social media tools. He even had an iPhone app (with a nifty "donate now" popup) that gave voters access to an Obama-branded play-by-play of the campaign. His YouTube videos got 110 million views and garnered an estimated 14.5 million hours of viewing. It's estimated that mass media advertising to reach that many viewers would have cost the Obama campaign $47 million.

On Facebook Obama attracted five million fans; his opponent, John McCain, one million. On MySpace Obama outpaced McCain by six hundred thousand fans. On Twitter he had more than one hundred thousand followers, compared to McCain's five thousand.[1]

People everywhere plugged their shiny gadgets into Obama's campaign because he was *speaking their language* (technology) and meeting them in the places *they gathered* (online). He was plugged in and relevant. Though it's likely Obama wasn't personally tweeting or answering e-mails, he *appeared* to be engaged and connected, which proved to be of central value to voters—a value greatly underestimated by Republicans. Obama's use of technology built an unmistakable, powerful brand that translated to influence in the voting booth.

Obama was plugged in and relevant.

Andrew Rasiej, cofounder of TechPresidents, a technology and politics Web site based in New York City, noted in *Wired* about Obama's campaign that politicians' growing awareness of the power of social networks and Internet tools will transform the business of politics "in the same way that the realization that the earth is round transformed the maritime industry."[2]

The world is mobilizing countless causes, platforms, and messages online. The U.S. Army, Navy, and Coast Guard have Facebook and Twitter accounts to reach out to future recruits and keep families updated about members of these services. Pope Benedict XVI has an iPhone app. He is also on Facebook and has a YouTube channel, as does Billy Graham (the Billy Graham Evangelistic Association).

a human space

As far back as 2002, Pope John Paul II got it. He understood the significance of the Internet and inspired Christians around the globe to embrace it as a way to share Christ with the world. Here's what he said in a public speech: "From this galaxy of sight and sound will the face of Christ emerge and the voice of Christ be heard? For it is only when His face is seen and His voice heard that the world will know the glad tidings of our redemption. This is the purpose of evangelization. And this is what will make the Internet a genuinely human space, for if there is no room for Christ, there is no room for man...I dare to summon the whole Church bravely to cross this new threshold, to put out into the deep of the Net, so that now as in the past the great engagement of the Gospel and culture may show to the world, 'the glory of God on the face of Christ.'"[3]

the speed of light

The reach of social networking is inestimable. The digital revolution has changed disaster recovery efforts forever. Social networks proved critical in the minutes and hours following the devastating earthquake in Haiti in January 2010. Social networking became lifelines for people trying to get information about loved ones as traditional communication channels failed. For the first time in the history of global tragedies, nearly $32 million was donated to the Red Cross using mobile phone texts.[4] Within hours of the May 2010 Nashville flood, volunteers mobilized and donations poured in, in large part due to the speed and agility of social networks.[5]

the body as a game changer

Much of social media's thrust, while old news to the tech crowd, is still finding its wings in nonprofits, businesses, government, schools, homes, and churches.

The good news: the church has momentum online.

The good news: the church has momentum online. Church leaders are starting to explore sharing the gospel through social networking channels. Pastors, youth leaders, missionaries, paraministries, artists, worship leaders, and writers are putting out compelling content, building networks, and making inroads for the Kingdom every day online. More and more churches include social networking time in their overall outreach efforts, and a growing number of churches are now fully online and attracting hearty online congregations.[6]

Communication channels have radically changed since Moses walked down the mountain, stone tablets in hand. Old Testament scribes wrote on parchment made from the treated skins of sheep or goats, and they used pens fashioned from reeds. The prophets preached in synagogues and countrysides. Later, Paul wrote his letters on scrolls of papyrus and gave them to slaves who would deliver them to the churches in other cities.[7]

Little did Paul realize the frenzy that would kick up on the other side of his prison bars as game changers emerged, ready to take up the charge of the gospel Generations of followers communicated the gospel with various tools. In 1440 the printing press changed everything as Bibles went from locked archives to retail. In 1517 Martin Luther nailed the Ninety-Five Theses on the door of the *Generations communicated the gospel with various tools.* University Church in Wittenberg and changed the game. Religious literature tracts were used as major channels throughout the turbulence of the Protestant Reformation in a movement that became known as "Tractarianism."[8] John Calvin wrote, debated, and preached tirelessly during the Reformation In the eighteenth century, John Wesley traveled 250,000 miles by horseback in his efforts to spread the Word, and he preached in open fields to as many as twenty thousand people at a time.

In 1922 Aimee Semple McPherson preached what is believed to be the first radio sermon. Christian writers such as A. W. Tozer shaped the faith during the Great Depression and C.S. Lewis followed with critical writings through WWII. Passionate game changers such as Dwight Moody, Oral Roberts, and Billy Graham also shared the gospel over the radio waves. Television and revivals catapulted the reach of Graham's ministry. His first televised crusade generated 1.5 million letters to the television station, confirming the power of that medium.[9]

In 1933 Dawson Trotman fervently pursued the goal "to know Christ and make Him known," and founded The Navigators, which began to mobilize college campuses to share the gospel. The spark was lit and soon the student-founded InterVarsity Christian Fellowship made its dent nationwide in the 1940s, via a movement that began earlier in England.

In the 1950s Bill and Vonette Bright changed the game when they founded Campus Crusade for Christ and ignited student evangelism on university campuses *internationally*. Bill Bright amplified the gospel's reach when he wrote the *The Four Spiritual Laws*, the most widely distributed religious booklet in history, and later commissioned *The JESUS Film*, one of the most influential films ever made. The renowned documentary on the life of Christ has reached more than 6 billion people in 234 countries and has been translated into one thousand languages. Campus Crusade is now the largest Christian organization in the world with ministries in 191 countries. It continues to make an impact taking evangelism online with Global Media Outreach (http://www. globalmediaoutreach.com/), a 24/7 equipping station designed to help others share the good news of Christ online.[10]

Since the 1990s writers such as Mark Kellner (*God on the Internet*) and Andrew Careaga (*E-Vangelism: Sharing the Gospel in Cyberspace*), opened the conversation for sharing the gospel in the online world. That conversation continues to gain momentum in churches and ministries around the globe.

> *Every day, people arise in the church with a message of hope.*

The list of dedicated, tireless evangelists seizing the communication vehicles of their days goes on, and on, and on. Today the Internet is just one more medium for ministers (with and without pulpits) to reach the masses—now globally—with the gospel. If you log on to Twitter, MySpace, Skype, or Facebook, you will find daily Bible studies, worship, and prayer sessions. More and more churches stream live sermons on Sundays that reach countless millions. People in countries previously shut off from the gospel are finding creative ways through mobile phones to access and share God's Word.

Online fund-raising has unleashed new possibilities for location-based missionaries who have embraced audio-blogging, podcasting, Flikr, and YouTube to build awareness for their work worldwide.

New leaders are emerging every day to lead this charge within the church. To learn more about the leaders, ministries, and churches, go to the resources tab at http://www.stickyjesus.com/. Also, check out our blog roll, located on the right-hand side of the site, to explore additional blogs making an impact online.

Some churches have purchased digital real estate in virtual worlds online and are holding regular church services. Second Life is a virtual world on the Internet in which "residents" create an identity, meet people, buy land, and build their own environment or purchase an existing one. It is a massively multiplayer online role-playing game (MMORPG), which offers *users* total freedom to create and interact as if they were living an alternate life online. Are your eyebrows raised? As strange as it sounds, real people behind the avatars are learning about and accepting Christ.[11]

The skies are alive with revelation and God's purposes rolling out over wireless networks. Every day, people arise in the church with a message of hope, and social networks have fit nicely into God's plan to mobilize His church.

a mobilized body—steve's story

Profile: Steve Berger, senior pastor, Grace Chapel, Leiper's Fork, Tennessee. Equipping people to be passionate servants of Jesus Christ.

Tools: Facebook, Ning, YouTube, Twitter.

Links: Learn more about Have Heart by visiting http://www.haveheart.net/, or visit Grace Chapel at http://www.gracechapel.net/. Follow @steve_berger on Twitter.

When Vanderbilt Medical Center was on the other end of the phone, my wife, Sarah, and I knew it wasn't good news. In Nashville, Vanderbilt is where the difficult cases go. We had many calls summoning us to Vanderbilt to comfort and help people in our congregation (Grace Chapel) and other friends. This time it was our turn.

Three days after the call from Vanderbilt, on his nineteenth birthday, we released our son Josiah Berger to heaven. The story, and what God taught us through this trial, is captured in our book *Have Heart: Bridging the Gulf Between Heaven and Earth.*

There was an immediate whirlwind surrounding this event. The staff at Vanderbilt Medical Center said they had never seen anything like it in all their years of operation. Hundreds of people began showing up at the hospital as the news of Josiah's accident began to circulate. And more were on their way by the time the first morning rolled around. People were everywhere—on the floor, in the chairs, and on the steps of the small chapel altar.

How did these people get the news about Josiah?

Certainly by traditional means, but by far, many people came as a result of social media, especially Twitter and Facebook. Plus, tens of thousands were "present" because of these tools and the regular updates they found on their friends' pages and within the "hashtag" stream. The power of social media, people's circle of friends, and technology came together and provided constant news about Josiah and our family.

The Twitter hashtag system of aggregating—or separating out a particular Twitter topic—became an important element in distributing news. The hashtag #JosiahBerger was used by hundreds of on-site people to update others around the world constantly. Tweeting (and retweeting) spread the news as close to instantly as possible. Talk about a worldwide prayer chain—our family had people everywhere not just concerned about Josiah, but actively praying and supporting us all as a result of hashtag and other regular updates!

Josiah has a Facebook page, and people continued to comment on his page just to feel close (and to express their support) to him and to us during the three-day vigil.

Social networking, in this instance, tremendously helped people feel a part of this incredible story. It provided, in real time, nearly instant access for people to be involved, lend their support, and come alongside us, even if those people were halfway around the world.

Facebook continues to be a channel as friends write loving thoughts to Josiah on his wall. With the release of our book, we've created a Have Heart Web site that includes a Ning community. The independent social network is housed on the site and is a member forum that allows people all over the world to come together digitally and share their stories of heaven and dive deeper into their collective understanding. The daily revelations shared by people, many of whom we've never met, continue to amaze us.

Tweeting spread the news as close to instantly as possible.

It's no secret. We believe Josiah's passing to heaven was God's divine green light to Sarah and me to change the game; to remove the intense sorrow, cultural tradition, and, yes, even the dreadful, finite language that has come to define the end of someone's earthly life. We want to ignite in others a passion for what God's Word says about heaven so they, too, can receive and live daily in that incredible hope. We long to see all Christ followers less and less attached to this world and more ready and excited about our eternal dwelling place! Social networking will continue to play a part in igniting a heaven revolution and communicating God's truth about eternity to others online.

you as a game changer

With today's technology, you can reach in minutes the physical ground that Paul and other game changers covered in years. Like Paul, each one of us can use God's Word to teach, warn, motivate, and inject God's perspective into popular culture.

Like Paul, you can share your life and how God is moving in it. You can mobilize people to pray, to give, to rebuild, to extend hope, and to step forward with the fresh revelation and power that God promised each and every one of us.

It is mind-blowing how instantly you can communicate a need, connect others to it, and rally a tidal wave of genuine support from people all over the world.

how to be a game changer online

✓ Pray for yourself. Ask God about the best way to share what He is showing you.

✓ Make it your business to know God's Word. Use Scripture in context, and share with others what it means to you, as the need arises.

✓ Share your passion for biblical knowledge in a *conversational* way with others.

✓ Use a variety of resources as references. Provide friends and followers with relevant resources or links, such as sermons, videos, and blog posts that may instruct or inspire them.

✓ Respect, love, and listen to the people in your online communities. Recognize that they, too, have words of life to share with you. The best teachers are the teachable ones.

✓ Use open-ended questions to spark deeper conversation. Doing so will help you gauge what's on the hearts and minds of people in your community.

✓ Be honest and transparent.

✓ Build a strong, sincere, online rapport with others. You need a relationship with others before they will give you permission to speak into whatever is going on in their lives.

✓ Be kind and keep a casual tone so you can lovingly challenge other believers in a nonthreatening way, especially if you are concerned about the theology they're promoting or their conduct online.

✓ Use direct messages (DM) to address sensitive situations. Take any issues you may have with a brother or sister in Christ to a private conversation.

✓ Always come from a heart of discipleship, not judgment. It's impossible to love people if you are busy judging them.

✓ Scan your favorite blogs, Facebook, and Twitter streams for people reaching out. Help them any way you can to be encouraged and press on.

✓ Don't get overwhelmed "doing." Pray. Then trust God to do the heavy lifting.

✓ Bring your faith-based perspective to conversations during local or global tragedies such as random violence, earthquakes, floods, and war. Your words can be powerful and bring hope to seemingly hopeless situations.

✓ If you can't find the words to say yourself, find a wise pastor or writer who is sharing his or her perspective online. You can find many great Christian leaders with perspective that you may wish to "borrow," but always remember to attribute your content. It is an honor to be an echo chamber for other men and women of God.

✓ Commit to learning new technologies and tools for online communication.

↻ download

↻ **Paul was a game changer. He stepped in and mobilized the Message.**

↻ **Paul knew how to keep it real. He wasn't afraid to show his transparency and human struggle.**

↻ **We can change culture one post, one tweet, and one community at a time.**

↻ **You can use the gospel to encourage, motivate, and mobilize.**

↻ **As a believer, you come from a long list of game changers. Now it's your turn.**

↻ **Are you ready to change the game?**

↻ upload

Dear Lord,

You alone ignite the hearts of ordinary men and women. You call them forth and commission them while they sleep. They are not radicals; they are not rebels. They are Christ followers. As Your holy eyes scan the fields, let them land on me. Find me worthy to carry Your message and Your promise to Your beloved creation. Find me trustworthy to step up and stand up in the moments when it matters most. Give me a holy boldness to change the game in my family, my community, and in this world for You, Jesus. Bless my steps and choose my battles as I advance as a game changer for Your glory. I vow to stand always on the authority of Your name and in the shadow of Your fame. Amen.

file 08 warning: danger zones

> **@stickyJesus** It's going to be hard, but I am with you.

The title of this file is a bit misleading. You really can't relegate danger to a "zone" online. An alarm won't go off if you get too close to a danger zone, nor will a crossing guard wave you through when the coast is clear. Danger is everywhere because we live on a broken planet.

While your message as a follower of Christ is grace, hope, and healing, there's a power that works equally hard online (and off-line) to cancel out your message by generating a perpetual flow of despair, hate, and evil.

Charli Pickett, blogger and cofounder of Shiloh Ministries, Inc., calls attention to the danger zones online and offers a prophetic interpretation of Jeremiah 9:20–21 (NIV) this way:[1]

> *Now, O women, hear the word of the LORD;*
> *(women, guardians of your family's heart,*
> *you are the chosen messengers*
> *of God's impending judgment)*
> **open your ears to the words of his mouth**
> *(apply God's Word boldly and*
> *warn others of the crisis at hand).*
> **Teach your daughters how to wail;**
> **teach one another a lament**
> *(teach them to grieve—not accept—what's being lost).*

> *Death has climbed in through our windows*
> *and has entered our fortresses;*
> (the enemy has found his way into our homes
> through the windows of our computers.)
> *it has cut off the children from the streets*
> (glued to computers and video games,
> our children no longer play outside)
> *and the young men from the public squares*
> (unwise use of technology has caused men to overwork
> and sin in isolation, putting our families and
> spiritual fellowship in very real danger).

The Internet is many things. Much of it is good; much of it is not. It can be a streaming channel where hate, sex, sin, and division go viral in seconds. As long as there are people on earth, evil will always find his way in and put his flag in the ground. It's why you need to get serious about infusing the Light and shaping this global meeting place for God's glory—sooner than later.

So dangerous or not, as with any nefarious mission field, it's time to log on and "go."

we're goin' in

If you set out on a mission trip into the depths of Papua New Guinea, you'd face scorpions, tigers, cholera, and people with spears who want to eat you. The mission field at your fingertips isn't so different. There's all of that and then some, metaphorically speaking.

While the Internet is the most powerful gateway to learning and profit that the world has ever seen, it's also *heaving* with darkness. So culture goes: what God creates for good, the enemy twists for his own evil purposes. You know the threats: pornography, infidelity, obscenity, theft, scams, slander, bullying, digital viruses, discrimination of every kind, cybercrime, physical violence, and even terrorism. All of this is no longer on the seedy, other side of town but just a few clicks away—in the cyber slums of the online city.

> *What God creates for good, the enemy twists for his own evil purposes.*

Studies show that our culture is literally living online, which is breeding serious problems. Excessive Internet use can weaken family bonds, create and feed online addictions such as gambling and shopping, increase emotional distress, and inhibit healthy socialization skills.[2] In the church this becomes an increasingly critical topic of discussion as leaders worry that online relationships will replace face-to-face discipleship and they respond to the fallout caused by online life.

So how can we avoid the blatant dangers online and discern the more subtle ones?

We put on our cyberarmor. We get off the well-worn path between church and home. We get real about what's going on in the culture around us and we refuse to be marginalized. We go to war.

"Be sober, be vigilant; because your adversary the devil walks about like a roaring lion, seeking whom he may devour."
1 Peter 5:8, NKJV

"My brethren, be strong in the Lord and in the power
of His might. Put on the whole armor of God,
that you may be able to stand against the wiles of the devil.
For we do not wrestle against flesh and blood,
but against principalities, against powers,
against the rulers of the darkness of this age,
against spiritual hosts of wickedness in the heavenly places."
Ephesians 6:10–12, NKJV

You know the score. The last thing the enemy wants to see is Jesus and His tribe of twenty-first-century, Internet-savvy followers gaining ground online. So he turns up the volume, complicates the simple, and amplifies the yammering so we don't know which way is up. He is the cultivator of fear, paranoia, and intimidation. He is the master of confusion and the king of anxiety. His goal is the same as it was in the garden. He exists to silence God's message of hope and genuine relationship with His children. Don't pick up the lies the enemy is putting down.

lies of the enemy

1. You are in the minority in the online world.

2. You are outvoted, outnumbered, and outranked here on earth.

3. Your faith is obsolete tradition rather than the God-breathed origin of humankind.

4. Your voice isn't relevant.

5. No one is listening to you.

6. Using social media is too hard, and you can't make a difference.

7. You're living in end times, and the online world is too lost to change. Why bother?

truths of God

1. Your inheritance includes the riches of heaven, and you belong to the holy majority *(1 Peter 1:4; 1 John 4:4)*.

2. As God's child, you've been given dominion and power over this earth *(Genesis 1:28)*.

3. The earth is the Lord's and everything in it (including the Internet). All things were created by Him and for Him *(1 Corinthians 10:26; Colossians 1:16)*.

4. The voice of Truth—His voice through you—is desperately needed in online conversations *(Psalm 78:6; Acts 1:8)*.

5. You carry a message that has transformed every generation since the beginning of time *(John 3:16; 2 Corinthians 4)*.

6. Everywhere you turn online, ears (and hearts) are burning for truth and hope. The world is morally and spiritually starving to death *(Isaiah 1; Matthew 5:14; Luke 5:31; Romans 5:8; 8:7–8; Philippians 2:15)*.

7. **We win** *(Job 19:25; Acts 1:11; 2 Thessalonians 2:8)*.

so get in the game

There's no turning back, sitting the bench, or asking the ref for a time-out. There is no ref and this game is perpetual. So get in shape. Check out the scoreboard: the numbers don't lie. More people will log on to blogs, Facebook, and Twitter this Sunday than will go to church. More people will meet the person they are going to marry online than will likely meet at the church barbecue. And more people will share their joys, heartbreak, and revelations via status updates than will seek the help of a counselor or a pastor this year.

It's your responsibility to influence the online conversation and to tell a clicking, texting, searching generation that they can't Google their eternal life.

To do this, you must master the tools needed to communicate the gospel to the world. And we've got to do it together. Currently, more than 33,820 denominations of the Christian faith exist.[3] Imagine if we could all get in the same pew for a few minutes. We could change everything.

As we discussed earlier, you need to be filled with and led by the Holy Spirit. That's a nonnegotiable part of the strategy. The Scriptures tell us in 1 Peter 1:13–16 to be holy, because God is holy. Even if we live in fast-moving, interactive environments, God is still at the center of that activity.

You can't do this in your own power. Nope. No way. Not a chance.

In Luke 4:1–14 when the Holy Spirit led Jesus to the desert and the devil tempted Him for forty days, Jesus used the words of God to claim His ground again and again. He defeated the devil in the desert with truth, and He will defeat the devil on-line—and in every seedy corner of cyberspace—using followers unafraid to stand firm and speak truth.

> *You can't do this in your own power.*

keys to resisting online temptation

You should not log online—or even get out of bed for that matter—without settling a very specific truth in your heart. And that is this: greater is He who is in you than the liar who is in the world (see 1 John 4:4).

take a heart stand

The Rock—Jesus Christ—cannot be overthrown. *You* can be overthrown, but there is no way that *He* can be overthrown. The good news? You belong to Him. Explore what it means to *abide* (to wait, dwell, and continue firmly) in Him. Jesus warned that this world would be packed with trouble and that His followers would be directly in the line of fire. But He finished that thought with a promise you can stand on: "Take heart! I have overcome the world" (John 16:33, NIV).

Even with your intentions pure and willpower praiseworthy, you aren't being scored on your performance. This is war and the prize is your soul. Without the Holy Spirit fighting this battle, you're dead.

"'Not by might nor by power, but by My Spirit,' says the LORD."
Zechariah 4:6, NKJV

connect with Him

Be in daily communion with God. Read His Word. Get on your face before you get on Facebook and seek before you tweet.

Let God's Word be your first download, His heart be your first search, and your praise to Him be your first upload of the day.

To pursue this more, read 1 Corinthians 9:27 and 1 Peter 1:13–15. A nourished heart is led by the Holy Spirit and knows instinctively when it's stepping onto shaky digital ground.

know your content

Every effective minister of the gospel (ordained or not) *knows* the Word of God. Jesus knew the Scriptures and could resist the devil. Paul studied before taking his ministry on the road. King Solomon mastered the Word and used it to lead Israel. Isaiah, Samuel, David, and John knew (and lived) the Word, and it changed the world.

"All Scripture is God-breathed and is useful for teaching,
rebuking, correcting and training in righteousness, so that the man
of God may be thoroughly equipped for every good work."
2 Timothy 3:16–17, NIV

"Your word is a lamp to my feet and a light for my path."
Psalm 119:105, NIV

"How can a young man keep his way pure?
By living according to your word.
I seek you with all my heart;
do not let me stray from your commands.
I have hidden your word in my heart
that I might not sin against you."

Psalm 119:9–11, NIV

"Get rid of all moral filth
and the evil that is so prevalent and humbly accept
the word planted in you, which can save you."

James 1:21, NIV

trust God to transform you

Ephesians 4:24 instructs you to walk transformed—as a new creation in Christ. That means you surrender and let the Lord do all the heavy lifting, or transforming. You are to separate from the bondage of old habits, thoughts, and behaviors—spiritually and mentally—*in His power*. Scripture says literally to "put on the Lord Jesus Christ" before you step (or click) into the world (Romans 13:14, NKJV). You pursue the likeness of Christ. Sure, it's a lofty goal, but you must remember that holiness is a process, not an event.

Romans 12:2 (NKJV) challenges you not to "be conformed to this world, but be transformed by the renewing of your mind." The English word *transformed* originates in the Greek from *metamorphoo*, from which we get the English word *metamorphosis*, meaning a gradual change. This change is made possible only by the Holy Spirit and daily meditation on God's Word.[4] When you are online, you surrender your need to be approved by people, and you walk in a way that honors God. This includes the way you dress, the language you use, the profile information you post, and the tone and spirit of the links you share.

"Am I now trying to win the approval
of men, or of God?
Or am I trying to please men?
If I were still trying to please men,
I would not be a servant of Christ."

Galatians 1:10, NIV

worship

That's right. Belt it out and let it loose! Allow God's presence to turn your mind into a citadel where the devil can't get in and where holiness can grow uninhibited. Surround yourself with worship music, listen to sermons and Bible readings, and worship with other believers every chance you get. Praise Him because He is awesome with no thought of blessing. Doing these things will cultivate an anointed mind and help you actively resist the temptations around you.

Beaten and bloodied, Paul and Silas began worshipping around midnight in their prison cell; they were praying and singing hymns. They worshipped God because they thought He was awesome. Worship busted them out. The earth shook, chains broke, and the prison doors blew open wide. Acts 16:26 says that *all* the prison doors were opened and *everyone's* chains fell off. If worship blesses God, breaks our chains, *and* can set the people around us free, then we need to get busy praying and singing!

go digitally dark

Log off and rest—often. Rest your mind, your eyes, and your thoughts. Rest your senses that have consistently absorbed images, sounds, and streaming ideas. Recoup, regroup, and pray. God did it on the Sabbath to teach us how to slow down and listen. He knew how your life would unfold and how living in the Land of Shiny Things would wear you out. You were created for simple, meaningful encounters with your Creator. From that rest will flow your worship, work, enthusiasm, energy, ideas, and vision. General George Patton was onto something when he said, "Fatigue makes cowards of us all."

Living in the Age of the Internet makes the godly issue of rest even more urgent.

"My Presence will go with you, and I will give you rest."
Exodus 33:14, NIV

"Come to me, all you who are weary and burdened, and I will give you rest. Take my yoke upon you and learn from me, for I am gentle and humble in heart, and you will find rest for your souls. For my yoke is easy and my burden is light."
Matthew 11:28–30, NIV

protect the family bond

By definition, protect means "to cover or shield from exposure, injury, damage, or destruction." Sounds like a war doesn't it? That's because it is. The enemy has come to destroy the family unit—and he'll use anything including the lure of shiny time online to do it. Your family is like a sanctuary; you must guard it like a soldier guards a fortress. With Americans spending nearly a quarter of their time online on social networking sites and blogs[5], you can bet that the family is getting the short end of the stick in the Land of Shiny Things.

It is never okay to let your time in online communities take away from precious (irreplaceable) time from the people God has entrusted to your care. We've all done it. As Christ followers, we must stand apart in the Land of Shiny Things. We must set the bar higher. Remember, you will answer for how you did (and did not) spend your time. Ask God constantly to help you be disciplined in this area and to model online boundaries for others. Set a timer, follow a plan, and talk candidly with your family about online ground rules for *everyone* (teens especially) in the home.

The enemy has come to destroy the family unit.

pursue and honor fellowship

Fellowship with those in the family of God is a surefire way to actively resist the enemy's snares. In fact, fellowship chases off the devil like a junkyard dog.

Online relationships will never replace the power of face-to-face (f2f) fellowship with other believers. Scripture tells us specifically to never fail to meet together (Hebrews 10:25). Why? Because incredible things happen when you gather with other people of faith. Look at the book of Acts: our perspective, power, and potential literally multiply when we faithfully come together. The disciples ate, worshipped, witnessed, and met together habitually with "glad and sincere hearts" (Acts 2:46, NIV).

That kind of fellowship, you can bet, takes logging off and making eye contact. It takes being present in the moment and joyfully forgoing any kind of gadget that diminishes the physical presence and worth of another person in front of you.

establish accountability

Don't skip this part. The need for weekly accountability with another person, a small group, or a spouse is critical. Balance your online and off-line lives.

Discuss the victories and the concerns in your online communities so that isolation or a "separateness" between the two worlds—virtual and face—doesn't compete for your attention.

If you have kids, be their accountability—every day. Ask them what's happening online, what friends they are talking to, and how they feel about what's being said. Make sure you have their passwords to social sites so you can check on the content and tenor of their online interactions.

> *"Let us consider how to stir up one another*
> *to love and good works, not neglecting to meet together,*
> *as is the habit of some, but encouraging one another,*
> *and all the more as you see the Day drawing near."*
> Hebrews 10:24–25, ESV

value your personal time

Chances are, if you were told you had only a week to live, you wouldn't spend your last precious hours surfing, clicking, and LOLing. Living in the Land of Shiny Things extracts all sense of time. We won't give our kids an hour of our time, but we'll putter three hours away trying to organize and post all of our photos (of our kids) to Facebook.

It's easy to lose track of—and devalue—the precious gift of time. The Internet can be a time thief. What you think will take a few minutes takes an hour. Your family has come to expect your just-a-sec-finger-raised-eyes-down posture as code that really means come-back-inside-we're-not-leaving-anytime-soon.

As a Christ follower, you have a responsibility to be a good steward of the time God has gifted you. If you have to, set a kitchen timer next to your computer or phone. Or purchase time control software that will literally kick you off your computer at specific times.

Study after study shows the physical and emotional impact of overindulging in technology. The risks include memory loss, impatience, fatigue, diminished eyesight, carpal tunnel syndrome, hand and back problems, and even depression.

Web sites like http://www.netaddiction.com/ and http://virtual-addiction.com/ offer self-assessment tests to help you determine whether technology has become your drug of choice. The site identifies at-risk people with questions such as: Do you neglect housework to spend more time online? Have you ever lied to cover up the amount of time you spend online? Are you frequently checking your e-mail? Do you often lose sleep because you log in late at night? If you answered "often" or "always" to any of these, technology may be taking a toll on you. Stay alert. The enemy will turn something good into something toxic.

be alert

The enemy knows that if he can capture your thought life, everything else will soon tumble down around you. Christ died to give you holiness, but the enemy aggressively and enthusiastically bets against your holiness before you've even had your first cup of coffee. So he throws vile images, videos, advertisements, television shows, movies, song lyrics, and memories of the past at you every chance he gets.

Life on this side of heaven is hard. Being online or off-line doesn't alter the degree of difficulty that is inherent to the human condition. It's never the hardware—the gun, the knife, the Internet—that causes a man to sin; it's the heart. Every day you will face another round in the ring. But if you go into each fight knowing it's your arm that will be raised as the champ, then the fight is just another chance to see God glorified in the midst of a world spilling over with temptation.

Remember the cross and how it defeated the sin in your life for good. You are no longer the underdog or a slave to the strongholds that left you hopeless. Jesus came as your escape route from all of the things you fear.

This isn't a pep talk. It's truth that must be settled in your heart here and now so that you can survive—and thrive—in this digital land. You must keep your mind and eyes fixed on the cross and all that Jesus accomplished on your behalf.

"We do live in the world, but we do not fight in the same way the world fights. We fight with weapons that are different from those the world uses. Our weapons have power from God that can destroy the enemy's strong places. We destroy people's arguments and every proud thing that raises itself against the knowledge of God. We capture every thought and make it give up and obey Christ."
2 Corinthians 10:3–5, NCV

declare war

Jesus actually yelled at His beloved disciple Peter, "Get behind Me, Satan!" (Matthew 16:23, NKJV) when Peter argued with God's plan. Sometimes to resist temptation actively, you have to get up and audibly declare your ground for Christ. Just the name of Jesus is enough to make the enemy flee your home, your office, your mind—or your laptop. Don't get comfortable with or glaze over the enemy's daily goal to steal, kill, and destroy you. That's a declaration of war that requires a stand from you daily.

God will never leave you to your own strategies. He is your resistance specialist, having earned His stripes in much larger battles on your behalf. He comes to your aid with a divine plan each day—if you respond with a willingness to obey and follow.

a matter of life and death

Living in the Land of Shiny Things and being more socially connected can be *deadly*. According to the National Safety Council, a 2010 study revealed that 28 percent of traffic accidents occur when people talk on cell phones or send text messages while driving. The vast majority of those crashes, 1.4 million each year, are caused by cell phone conversations, and 200,000 can be blamed on text messaging, according to the report. The increase in text messages sent per minute is dramatic: text messages have gone from 319 per minute in 2000 to over 2.5 million in 2008. [6]

gadget ground rules

❖ Commit to staying off the phone when you're on the road. That means no texting, no checking for messages, no reading e-mails, and no talking.

❖ Use a cell phone in a car only when the car is safely parked.

❖ Put the cell phone in the glove box if you can't resist the urge to check it while driving. Remember, by engaging with your gadgets while driving, you are teaching your children to do the same thing.

❖ Eliminate the distractions for your teen. If your state doesn't have laws banning cell phone usage while driving, then you ban it from your teen's car.

safety online—it's a big deal

The Internet never forgets. Never.

It is the world's largest information exchange...and filing cabinet. Only post profile information or share content with others that you don't mind the whole world seeing…and possibly sharing. More and more often, employers, colleges, and potential business associates are checking the minutiae of social networking sites to inform very big decisions.

If you are going to be online, be alert and be smart about the information you share. If you have kids online, triple that warning.

quick tips to be safe (and smart) online

✓ Don't post personal information such as your home address, your phone number, or the town in which you live.

✓ Restrict access to your Facebook page only to people you know. Go to privacy settings and switch your settings to "friends only." Do the same for your kids' pages.

✓ Be modest if you post a photo. Ask yourself: Would my mom frame this and put it on her piano? Better yet, would Jesus carry it in His wallet and show it off to others? Be aware that photos can also be digitally modified.

✓ Take a friend and always go to a public place when you meet someone off-line for the first time. If you can't take a friend, let someone else know where you are going, when you will return, and details about the person you are meeting.

✓ Speak frankly to your teen about the dangers of online predators and why face-to-face meetings are prohibited. A full list of online safety issues to discuss with kids and teens specifically can be found at StickyJesus.com.

✓ Don't nurture inappropriate conversations with the opposite sex if you are married and belong to social networks. Avoid being tempted—and tempting. If you are single, be especially careful not to divulge too much personal information. Pace your interactions, and remember, you are interacting not with profiles but with real people.

✓ Don't tweet or post information that reveals your husband will be away for three days or that you can't wait to leave for vacation tomorrow. Post vacation photos when you return.

✓ Don't advertise expensive items for sale on eBay, Craigslist, or any other social network, because you may attract the wrong kind of customer. A person intent on committing a crime will find ways to track down a physical address.[7]

blocking unwanted content

Thankfully, a number of filtering software solutions exist on the market that give you control over incoming content. Safe Eyes (we like it because it's for PC and Mac; go to http://www.internetsafety.com/) blocks questionable content and allows time limits and full reporting of online activity. Recovery groups dealing with pornography and sex addiction also use the software for accountability purposes. Safe Eyes, and software like it, issues instant alerts to a parent, spouse, or accountability partner if a user attempts to access a blocked site. It also issues daily usage reports that show time online, Web sites visited, and the full text of IM conversations. For social networking, the software will catch and block inappropriate postings and videos and block access to entire networks. There are also phone and iPod apps that block content and control texting.

Visit http://www.stickyjesus.com/ for a comprehensive list of organizations and Web sites committed to help you and your family stay safe online.

⟳ download

- ⟲ **The Internet is loaded with cyber slums and danger zones.**

- ⟲ **You need to know what is going on in the culture around you.**

- ⟲ **Satan's goal is to silence God's message of hope to the world.**

- ⟲ **God has given you dominion over the shiny things of this earth and the Internet.**

- ⟲ **Hearts are hungry for the message you carry.**

- ⟲ **Guard your heart, mind, and time online.**

- ⟲ **Log off. Rest. Often.**

- ⟲ **Set family ground rules for online time. Model the higher standard.**

- ⟲ **Never text and drive. Never.**

- ⟲ **Protect yourself and your family from unwanted content with filtering software for your computer and your gadgets.**

⌂ upload

Dear Lord,

I have beheld Your power and Your glory. The times we've shared together have planted a trust and an awe deep within me. I can trust You to guard my heart from anything coming my way today. When the storms come, You will enfold me in a safe place. You are holy, and I, too, desire to be holy. I claim my inheritance and walk boldly in the new life You've given me. I don't just believe in You, Lord; I believe You—every word and every promise. Therefore, I will never walk alone. Your Word is a lamp to my feet and to my thoughts in this dark land. I stand in Your power—and declare war against the accuser online today. You are the God that crumbled Jericho; the God who cracked open the sea; and the God who ripped the veil once and for all. There is nothing that can separate me from the power of Your love in the Land of Shiny Things. Nothing. Amen.

file 09 quiet: humility zone

> **@stickyJesus** My holiness trumps your awesomeness.

Share

You've come to know these words: *humility*, *service*, *simplicity*, and *love*. These words don't naturally fit into the online culture today. Still, these words define the life of a believer.

So there's the rub. And the reason that humility gets its very own file in the Land of Shiny Things.

Everywhere you click online, competing messages, philosophies, opinions, and personal agendas dominate. Being in the Land of Shiny Things can complicate rather than simplify the life of a believer...if you advance without caution. A majority, if not all, of the people online are talking, selling, exchanging information or goods, purchasing, or making a full-time job of persuading others to do something. It's a cultural currency that can heavily influence your thinking, vocabulary, perception, and self-image—like it or not, agree or not.

If you spend any time at all on social networks, you know there's a rock star or expert born every minute. You can't be online for five minutes without bumping into an all-star blogger, marketing maven, social networking ninja, SEO expert, or Hollywood celebrity dueling for the number one spot in the online conversation. People will say a lot of things—both true and liberal versions of true—to gain and maintain those titles.

It's the land of streaming me.

The online culture provides the perfect storm for pride to rise up like a toxic tsunami. To quote C. S. Lewis, "Humility is not thinking *less of* yourself but thinking of yourself less." When you think more of yourself, you create a place where pride creeps in, and if you're not careful, it finds a place to set up permanent residence deep inside you. (By the way, pride doesn't mind sharing the neighborhood with fear.)

In Romans 12:9–16 (RSV) Paul urges believers to "let love be genuine" and not to "be haughty, but associate with the lowly; never be conceited." And in Galatians 6:14 (NIV) he identifies the one and only thing we should ever be arrogant about: "May I never boast except in the cross of our Lord Jesus Christ, through which the world has been crucified to me, and I to the world."

As a believer, you're suspended between two worlds when you log online. Marketers are in the business of pushing your hot buttons—the emotional wires that, when tripped, just might make you want to buy, buy, and buy things. Hot buttons are needs and desires we all have for things like control, status, and fun. Marketers know your needs, and it's their job to satisfy them with a better idea, product, or service. If they can get you to become preoccupied (and even obsessed) with your needs, then they own your mind and your pocketbook. And if you have a large social network, they've likely managed to influence some of your friends too. Does this make marketers evil? No. It just lumps them in with the rest of humankind destined to toil creatively for food and shelter.

By now it's clear the language of this mission field isn't Swahili, Arabic, or Thai. It's fame and significance. For the Christian trying to figure out how to be *in* this world but not *of* this world, the online culture presents an ever-present conflict. The 24/7 push and pull of information generates the me-centric environment rife with emotional land mines. Keeping a steady hand on pride and learning how to separate the wheat from the chaff (the useful from the useless) become the street smarts necessary to keep prideful behaviors at bay.

guard your heart

It takes absolute intention and diligence to guard your heart in this world online or off-line. If you let pride in, it will seize every opportunity to separate you from others and, more importantly, from God. God's Word is straight up when it comes to pride.

"God has had it with the proud,
but takes delight in just plain people."
1 Peter 5:4, THE MESSAGE

"First pride, then the crash—the bigger the ego, the harder the fall."
Proverbs 16:18, THE MESSAGE

"Do you want to stand out? Then step down. Be a servant.
If you puff yourself up, you'll get the wind knocked out of you.
But if you're content to simply be yourself,
your life will count for plenty."
Matthew 23:11–12, THE MESSAGE

pride: what it looks like

In the book *Lead Like Jesus: Lessons from the Greatest Leadership Role Model of All Time*, authors Ken Blanchard and Phil Hodges provide an in-depth look at pride, saying that pride centers on the promotion of self.[1] It is, as we read in Romans 12:3 (NIV), "think[ing] of yourself more highly than you ought." We've called out some of the characteristics from their list and applied them to the online environment.

pride does all the talking

Pride takes credit, demands attention, boasts, shows off, or demands something because of who you are.

By staying close to the famous One, you can guard your heart against pride and keep so much of *you* from dominating so much of everyone else. It's rare that people will tell you when they see you "overdoing you," but be assured, they notice. (Perhaps it was the fiftieth profile photo you added in a week. Or, maybe it was the photo of you in your leather jacket next to your Porsche with your speedboat casually placed in the background.) The point is that too much "you" may close doors in others' minds that can never be reopened to the love of Christ. There will always be the posts or conversations about what you are doing and what you like. Those comments make you real and help you connect to others with like interests. It is when you start to drift into the "see me, aren't I great, don't I know all the right people, don't I make a difference?" zone that people will start to shut down.

pride ignores people

Pride considers others who are too far below you in position or credentials as not worthy of your support or the kindness of your follow.

Author Philip Yancey hit pride head-on when he said: "Whatever makes us feel superior to other people, whatever tempts us to convey a sense of superiority, that is gravity [of our sinful nature], not grace."[2]

Frankly, nothing says, "I don't get it," like a church, a pastor, an author, or a celebrity who has a Twitter following in the tens of thousands and then follows absolutely no one. Then there are others who will only follow the select few they want to follow. You hear them justify it by saying that it is just too hard to follow that many people. It can be overwhelming, indeed, to follow so many, but it shouldn't become an excuse for excluding others.

On Twitter, creating lists is an easy way to help you organize followers and keep track of people based on familiarity or interests. For those who do have a massive following, lists can also be made private so you don't have to feel as though you are offending anyone you've not included. Twitter.com provides instruction on how to organize your followers with lists (also see pg. 147).

Be ready to have your thinking and content challenged.

With Facebook and blogs, interaction is even more important because you have specifically accepted them as a friend or fan or provided a space that asks for comments. If someone takes the time to post a comment and it is never acknowledged, it is like a dropped call. If the conversation always stops and there is never an exchange, then a deeper connection doesn't happen. Over time frustration builds and people stop trying to engage. You have adequately sent the message that they don't matter.

pride acts above it all

Pride is aghast when someone dares to challenge its thinking. The rules, judgments, and standards you impose on others should not apply to you.

If you are going to step onto the field, you have to be ready to have your thinking and content challenged. How you receive feedback and challenges to your thinking will speak volumes about your heart. This doesn't mean you back down or don't defend your thinking. But don't quickly dismiss others because they obviously don't have your background or experience.

Keeping your heart open can make all the difference. You always have an opportunity to demonstrate grace in how you receive and how you disagree with others online. If you find yourself irritated because someone holds you accountable or challenges you directly, it is time for a heart check.

pride's image comes first

For the prideful person, image becomes more important than substance and truth. When this happens you find yourself fretful about what others think and how they respond to you. You worry about how an unkind comment to or about you will be perceived by others. You are tempted to modify what you do and how you do it, because you want to conform to what you think will be more popular. You may also start to behave inconsistently with who you are or how you really feel. You become vulnerable when you let others govern what you believe is right. When your image is your driving force, you start to slip down a dangerous slope.

pride judges

Pride sees the value of an idea based on *who said it* rather than the quality of the thought.

If you engage in social networking at any level, it's not long before you notice cliques, experience exclusion, or recognize that you are essentially invisible to some people. Yes, it can be like high school. Accept that this happens, and keep moving. Just don't be the one to initiate or feed the behavior, which is contrary to the mission.

Everyone is capable of a great idea or thought. If you find something great and only feel compelled to share it based on who it came from, then check yourself. The pride buzzer may be ringing. Inspired thinking can come from many places, and it is important to always attribute content to whoever developed it. A worthy idea is a worthy idea. Share the ones that matter and that reflect truth, not just the ones that come from a celebrity source. Let your heart guide you, not the position of the one who said it.

> *There's a lot of false humility going down online.*

humility: what it looks like

There's a lot of false humility and exaggerated speech going down online (remember, the undergirding value is to monetize you). So how do you discern the wayward voices? Carefully and prayerfully. The prophet Micah captured the essence of a life well lived. It is not surprising that the Old Testament book in his name discusses the characteristic of humility, particularly how it fits into our relationship with God.

"He has shown you, O man, what is good;
and what does the LORD require of you but to do justly,
to love mercy, and to walk humbly with your God?"

Micah 6:8, NKJV

humility reaches out

The easy path is to seek out people in life who are just like you; however, social networking provides the perfect opportunity to reach out to someone who is *not* like you. Humility finds someone outside its usual circle of friends. It may mean finding someone just getting started in social networking and being that hand that brings him or her along.

humility seeks to serve

Humility looks for opportunities to share what has been given. It will answer a simple tech problem, make a quick recommendation, or offer a resource that might be the perfect portal to sharing Truth in the future.

humility models gratitude

Humility is thankful and says thanks—often. It gives people a nod when kindness is extended. It is digitally generous. Humility acknowledges interactions, favors, referrals, prayer, and when value is shared.

humility has a gentle tone

Humility lifts others up. It doesn't condescend or diminish another person's value. It doesn't ignore, marginalize, or favor. It never criticizes or corrects in public, especially over minor things.

humility thinks less of self

Humility works on behalf of the Lord. Humility promotes His name and His fame over personal agendas. It talks little about itself. If it has written *another* book, received *another* award, given *another* donation, or had lunch with *another* famous person, it doesn't plug it—again. It doesn't drop names *repeatedly* in order to be elevated or affirmed. Humility listens, responds, and interacts rather than broadcasts. Humility understands that a little goes a long way.

Everyone has an ego. The Apostle Paul, Mother Teresa, Brother Lawrence, and Gandhi all had egos. God crafted you with a healthy amount of ego and installed an internal dial in your spirit that you can adjust at will. You see unmistakable ego in Jesus' disciples, which proves that even being in God's very presence isn't inoculation enough against the pitfalls of pride. You see—or perceive—pride more and more online as more Christian authors, speakers, musicians, pastors, and everyday social savvy Joes gain larger online followings. Christ followers are not immune to ego. We all fall prey to the persuasions of the culture and our own haunting *needs*—to succeed, to be accepted, to be loved, and to know we matter in the world.

What you have to remember when you fire up your cache of shiny gadgets each day is that Jesus Christ came to free you from the weight and the burden of *all that need*. Writer Andrew Murray says the only humility that is really ours is "not that which we try to show before God in prayer, but that which we carry with us in our daily conduct." So the goal of the saint is to live in *that place* as part of our intrinsic self. As John so vividly and visually explains the equation, we must decrease so that Christ may increase.

*"This is the assigned moment for him to move into the center,
while I slip off to the sidelines."*
John 3:30, THE MESSAGE

In dying to self you purge the weight of pride so there's actual real estate in your heart in which humility can live and grow. The origin of humility requires a metamorphosis of brokenness that can't be taught or passed from one person to another. It has to be reckoned with before the cross, submitted to in the presence of Christ, and rigorously pursued daily. In a spirit of humility you experience true freedom through Christ. It's a heavenly equation that can confound the people around you. The world can try to graph it, map it, debate it, and reframe it, and still, the most brilliant minds can't justify how true freedom comes from putting yourself last in the chain of command.

Does humility mean you can't express self-confidence? No, not at all. Just know there's a fine line between confidence and arrogance. Confidence can talk a lot, but that talk tends to inspire others and be concerned with igniting excellence in others. Arrogance tends to be self-absorbed and oblivious to the needs, insights, or aspirations of others.

Expertise, talent, and excellence are God-given and deserve to be recognized in this world. When a Christ follower displays excellence in his or her craft or talent, God is glorified in a powerful way, and the world takes note. However, when that recognition leads to *self-elevation*, it can be a problem. If you find yourself repeatedly gravitating toward applause or attention online, then it's a good indication you've lost sight of the mission. Know that God loves you too much to allow you to continue on that path for long without stepping in.

So check yourself. Living in the Land of Shiny Things releases a subtle elixir of false worth into the air that easily entices. Mercifully, God gives us His word to remind us that our most noble endeavors—while impressive to this world—will never draw heaven's applause if they lack the heart of humility, which is love.

clanging cymbal or beating heart?

"If I speak in the tongues of men and of angels, but have not love, I am only a resounding gong or a clanging cymbal. If I have the gift of prophecy and can fathom all mysteries and all knowledge, and if I have a faith that can move mountains, but have not love, I am nothing. If I give all I possess to the poor and surrender my body to the flames, but have not love, I gain nothing.
Love is patient, love is kind. It does not envy, it does not boast, it is not proud. It is not rude, it is not self-seeking, it is not easily angered, it keeps no record of wrongs. Love does not delight in evil but rejoices with the truth. It always protects, always trusts, always hopes, always perseveres. Love never fails."

1 Corinthians 13:1-8, NIV

humility—claire's story

Profile: Claire McLean is...alive 2 know God & make Him known... dreaming of revival...love Lost, preaching, Coca-Cola, loud music, funky rings, church, friends, my husband, my spunky kids...

Tools: Twitter, Facebook, blog.

Links: On Twitter follow Claire @fireball3316 and read her blog http://onepassiononedevotion.wordpress.com/.

It's amazing how a short tweet saying, "I'm praying for you," can open up a conversation that may affect eternity. Last year this happened in a really dramatic way for me. A Facebook friend put "I'm praying" as his status update one day. From what I had gathered from his profile information, this young guy wasn't a Christian and had been living a homosexual lifestyle. So, for him to write "I'm praying" was a sign that something more was going on.

I could have ignored it, but I didn't. I engaged and commented below his post, "I'm praying too," and asked him for details. He shared that his workmate had been rushed to the hospital and was expected to die of a brain hemorrhage and that only a miracle would save her. He also acknowledged that he thought I might be the only real Christian he knew or had any contact with.

God had connected us for such a time as this. It had the weight of *this is something big* on it.

Immediately I prayed for this young man. I prayed that God would heal his workmate and that this would show both of them that God is indeed real. Praise God! The workmate miraculously recovered, and the only answer this young man could give was that we had prayed and that a very real, powerful, supernatural God had intervened.

Do not be fooled. Much of the information on the Internet isn't so much about facts and data as it is about people's hearts and passions, and being able to communicate to *real* people about *real* life. Conversations range from the mundane and the humorous to the heartbreaking and the inspiring. Putting on the heart of Christ before I log online is about identifying with people, being intentional about forming real community, and building support networks designed to break the barriers of location and time zone.

To me, social networking is a gift from God to this generation. Being a blogger and being active in social networks such as Facebook and Twitter have opened up opportunities to share how God has helped me in my life. I love to encourage both believers and nonbelievers to discover how deep God's love is for them. Many times I have prayed in earnest for others, and they've prayed for me at critical times.

I first started blogging about five years ago as a way of processing what I was learning in life, in prayer, and in my personal study of God. I hoped that what I shared would help someone and be a springboard for him or her to draw closer to God. My life mission is to know God and make Him known, so plugging in to social media and blogging are natural extensions of that passion. Blogging is the ultimate power tool for my mission. From blogging I found Facebook and soon moved on to Twitter.

Social networking gets back to the instruction to be jars of clay for God to shine His glorious power, truth, and love through (2 Corinthians 4:7). Is doing that online hard? Not at all. There are times when I feel particularly moved to share a verse from the Bible, a quote, or just something from my heart that reflects how God speaks or moves daily. There is a well-known quote: "As Christians, we might be the only Bible someone ever reads."

One thing that amazed me about both social networking sites was it wasn't just about connecting with established friends, but it was also about having the courage to connect with strangers and make new friends worldwide, much like Paul and the other disciples did. I have made some real friends—and I do call them *real* friends—all over the world, from Ireland to the United States, Rarotonga, Australia, and Canada. It's like God is connecting His family all around the globe regardless of distance, language, race, or title.

> *He gets the whole applause— every last, stray clap.*

In my blog, I write about spiritual things or just random things I might be inspired or challenged by in my daily Christian walk. It is always humbling to receive a blog comment. Recently someone commented: "Your blog speaks everything that I never knew how to put into words." And another woman wrote: "Thank you. I needed this today."

Though I've been at this a while now, it still amazes me that the words I share from my heart—all the way from New Zealand—can reach the hearts of people on the other side of the world and be exactly the words they needed to hear.

the famous One

God doesn't need a costar, a coproducer, a casting director, or even well-meaning guys running lights. He's it. From opening act to encore, He's the whole show. And He gets the whole applause—every last, stray clap. If your heart and mind did not connect with the weight of that truth, please, read it again until it clicks...and before you click.

Jesus didn't *talk* about humility. He didn't have to. Jesus *was* humility. He saw—and sees—every sinner the same. Be it a congressman, a clergy member, or a crackhead—all are equally broken and equally beloved in His eyes. He knew that pride and arrogance would destroy the disciples' witness and that their very humanness worked against them. So He did something that would leave a lasting impression on them...and us.

Can you imagine what Simon Peter must have been thinking when Jesus began to wash the feet of His disciples (see John 13:1–17)?

⊙ let's go there...

It's scandalous! Peter thought as he watched Jesus—Israel's Messiah and King—kneeling down before each disciple and methodically washing the filth and grime from his feet. Without pretense or hurry, Jesus took their feet into holy hands and, with great love and intention, made them clean.

He looks like a slave hunched over like that...How could He stoop to this? Peter's eyes were frantic as they scanned the room. *What? No uproar? No protest? They are just going to let Him perform this lowly, despicable task? Am I the only one sober enough to see the paradox of a King stooped so low?* His heart was beating so fast, he fully expected it to leap from his flesh any moment.

This made no sense to Peter. Just days earlier, Jesus had ridden into Jerusalem on a donkey as the Messiah and fulfilled what Scripture had promised. "Hosanna! Hosanna!" the crowd had shouted as they placed palm branches on the road before Him.

Jesus had status, which meant that simply by association, so did Peter. Right?

Jesus was declared the Son of God, and Peter couldn't get close enough to Him that day. His heart had swelled with pride that he walked on the same road accompanying King Jesus. *There had been so many followers!* Peter thought. He loved looking at them all.

And now—the sight of Him. *I can't stand this...He looks like anyone else...so ordinary...almost like a peasant...a peasant with filthy hands! Get up,* Peter's heart begged silently. *Please, Master, get up before everyone sees You!* Peter nearly stopped breathing. *Don't come this way...please, please, don't.* But there He was. Jesus looked up into Peter's eyes. It was a point of view that Peter had never had in all the years he had been with Jesus. The King of heaven...looking up...at him. The awkward pause collided head-on with Peter's raging heartbeat. Peter pulled away from Jesus, refusing His gesture.

Instantly an acute awareness of his own sin flooded Peter's heart. Jesus' eyes said it all.

Will they ever get it? Will they ever release the unbearable weight of status, pride, and self? Will they ever exchange their anxious, striving hearts for My peace?

I have come to rescue you from your high and mighty, "me too" life whirling inside your head.

Come. Loosen your grip. Live.

It took him a minute, but Peter got it. In fact, in his zeal, he offered Jesus not only his feet to wash but also his hands and head! Jesus gave His disciples a love stamp that night, a visual they would have for the mission field forever. With a simple, profound act, Jesus poured out His love, affirmed their unity, and at the same time, stripped them of their exhausting quest for worldly rank and status. They were crowned and commissioned for the battle ahead, equipped and clothed in the humility of heaven's King.

⇩ download

↱ **There's only one who is truly famous, and His name is Jesus Christ.**

↱ **Love must define your mission online.**

↱ **Reach out, seek to serve, forgive, and be inclusive.**

↱ **Discern your tone to avoid the pitfall of pride.**

↱ **Jesus Christ came to free us from the heaviness and the burden of our unmet *need*.**

↱ **Humility is one of the most powerful weapons on earth.**

↱ **"For we do not preach ourselves, but Jesus Christ as Lord, and ourselves as your servants for Jesus' sake" (2 Corinthians 4:5, NIV).**

↱ **"For everyone who exalts himself will be humbled, and he who humbles himself will be exalted" (Luke 14:11, NIV).**

⇧ upload

Dear Lord,

You are Jehovah-M'Kaddesh, the God who sanctifies. Approve me Lord; set me apart for your work. Extract my hidden need and fill me with a worship that extinguishes pride. At times I am far too influenced by what others think of me. My words and actions inject a carnal clamor into a world that desperately needs to hear the sound of Your love. Forgive my need to know and be known and an agenda that siphons your applause. Lord, you despise the puffed up. I surrender my need to be served and heard. I need a holy transfusion of grace to save my life; nothing less will do. Send my agenda to the back of the line and soundproof my ears to the praise of this world. It's You and You alone that I seek, Lord. I want to tell your story in this digital sea of streaming "me." Take me to the secret place, Father, and forever I will praise you there. Amen.

file 10 cost: everything

> **@stickyJesus** For God so loved the world, He sent Me to save it.

Share

When God sent His Son to absorb the sins of the world, it cost Him everything. But with that grace came an inherent cost that attaches itself to the life of every Christ follower residing on earth.

It's what German-born pastor and theologian Dietrich Bonheoffer called "costly grace" in his book *The Cost of Discipleship*.[1] "Cheap grace is the preaching of forgiveness without requiring repentance," wrote Bonheoffer, while "costly grace is the sanctuary of God; it has to be protected from the world, and not thrown to the dogs." In other works Bonheoffer urged Christians "to share in the sufferings of God at the hands of a godless world if the church was to be a true reflection of Christ."[2]

That suffering implies standing up and standing apart, no matter the cost or consequence. For centuries Christians the world over have suffered for their faith. They've been ostracized, criticized, and in the case of so many, even put to death for what they believe. Although it's not likely you will endure such persecution, you will suffer for choosing to follow King Jesus.

into the flames

In the online world, you will encounter *trolls* (people who repeatedly post negative comments on blogs and social networks), *flamers* (people who incite and fuel arguments), *haters* (outspoken, anti-everything people), *blockers* (those who block you from Twitter if you make a mistake or touch a nerve), and *de-frienders* on Facebook (those out to teach you a lesson by hitting the "de-friend" button).

Online you will experience days of pure elation, God connection, and eternity-altering testimony. Then there are the *other days*—days of missteps, anxiety, self-doubt, rejection, and despair. They are the same experiences and emotions intrinsic to living in any community that includes human beings. You just need to know, the same can and will happen online.

But that's okay. You're on a mission.

We are not called to be accepted. We are called to glorify God.

As Pastor Paul Washer says, "We are not called to build empires. We are not called to be accepted. We are called to glorify God."[3] If you can keep that mindset and Jesus' encouragement etched in your heart, you're going to be fine.

"Blessed are you when they revile and persecute you,
and say all kinds of evil against you falsely for My sake.
Rejoice and be exceedingly glad, for great is your reward in heaven,
for so they persecuted the prophets who were before you."
Matthew 5:11–12, NKJV

walking the cyber aisle

At some juncture you will have to walk the cyber aisle. This means "coming out" that you are a Christian. Don't look so surprised. For some people, this can be terrifying. For others, expressing their faith looks like a slow coming out; they'll give you a little "Amen" here or a Scripture nod there. Others can stand on a mountaintop with a bullhorn and give a testimony that would make the wildlife repent. Wherever you are, remember that being set apart by God to be the light in this dark world is a good thing, *a very good thing.*

Because you love God, people are going to form instant opinions about you—some good, some not so much. You may alienate friends, annoy your neighbors, and even lose a job or family ties by loving God. There will be days when you are interacting online and you will feel lonely and shunned, and question whether you are making any difference at all. That's okay. It's the emotional cost of being a messenger of grace in a foreign land. Hear Paul's words:

"Let us not grow weary while doing good,
for in due season we shall reap if we do not lose heart."
Galatians 6:9, NKJV

turning down the world

Be honest: Do people have to ask if you're a Christian? Do your words, music, hobbies, jokes, attitude, and social commentaries make it hard to distinguish you as a follower of Christ?

In Revelation 3:16 (ESV) God warns us to be either hot or cold in our faith. Anything lukewarm and He says, "I will spit you out of my mouth."

Wow. That's kind of harsh, isn't it?

Not if you consider *His cost.*

Let's imagine that you sacrificed your kidney so your diabetic brother could live. Your decision was not an easy one and certainly not risk-free. Let's imagine after you gave him your kidney, your brother started drinking heavily, taking drugs, and eating all kinds of fatty foods. Would you get a little peeved?

> *A lukewarm Christian life hurts you and everyone in your path.*

Let's go a step farther. Let's imagine you sacrificed your son to save the life of another child trapped in a burning bus. After you carried the child to safety, you rushed back to get your son only the bus door jammed and you had to watch your child die a slow, horrific death. As hard as it is, let's imagine the years passing and you living each day with those images of your son's suffering. You hear his screams. You feel his pain.

Meanwhile, the child you saved has grown up and is living a self-absorbed life with little trace of gratitude. The person's words, actions, jokes, and relationships don't reflect the precious gift of life or the depth of *the exchange.* All of a sudden, spitting that person from your mouth becomes the kindest thing you could do.

These are dreadful pictures but not far-fetched if you want to keep it real about grace and gratitude. A lukewarm Christian life hurts you and everyone in your path. Mostly, it hurts the Father who created you. Not only is your own life disconnected from the power of the Holy Spirit, but it's likely you are seriously confusing the people around you. And for that, you'll be accountable someday.

Your degree of buy-in to the culture around you influences the way you appear in photos, talk, and interact with others online. It affects the content you download and the ideas and social views you upload. Think of it this way: if Christ lives in you, then anything you see or hear, the Holy Spirit also sees and hears, including music, movies, photos, videos, television, and every variety of conversation you consume.

heartbreak

You will see people use the word *Christian*, *Christ follower*, or *believer* to describe themselves in their profiles, in their status updates, or on their blogs. You will see Scripture quoted, prayers offered in earnest, and kind words exchanged. Then, you will see those same people speaking and acting as if they never met Christ. Some of these people may be pastors, ministry leaders, mentors, or people you've put on an earthly pedestal. You will see many believers intermingling new age beliefs, hodgepodge doctrines, racial jokes, and astrology references into their conversations. You will see young people disrespecting one another and their own bodies. You will see sides of people you love that you never anticipated. With access behind the curtains of people's lives comes the good, the bad, and the heartbreaking.

You are not alone. These are the same things that broke the hearts of Jesus, Moses, and Paul as they saw professed believers worshipping idols and blending in.

personal bandwidth

Impacting the online space for Christ will cost you time, energy, and maybe even money. You will have to invest time in order to "know your stuff" and mature as a student of the Scriptures. Doing this will prepare you for the conversations God entrusts to you. He desires that your knowledge of His Word grows and grows. Your part in that equation is to trust, His part is to do. Allow God to stir a fire in your heart to know Him and His Word more. It's that easy.

"I pray that your love will overflow more and more, and that you will keep on growing in knowledge and understanding."
Philippians 1:9, NLT

Following Christ and reaching out to others will also cost you time. It takes precious time to build relationships and to sow Truth into other people's lives. Make no mistake: you may live in an instant, gotta-have-it-yesterday world, but that hyperfast mentality can't be applied to nurturing Kingdom relationships. That means you will lose some "me" time as you invest yourself in others. It may also cost you money. The Holy Spirit may nudge you to send a book or CD to someone to encourage or teach. He may tell you to go visit someone in another city, donate to a mission trip, or directly help a person or family in need.

"a hundred times as much"

The cost of following Christ pales in comparison to the gift of grace you've inherited though the blood of Jesus Christ and the gift of eternal life. In the business world, this is where you might fire up the Excel spreadsheet and do a cost-benefit analysis. Only you wouldn't get very far. Our advice is to shut your computer down before all the "benefits" weighing down the right-hand column cause your system to crash. There simply isn't a way to calculate what love invested on earth renders in heaven.

There simply isn't a way to calculate what love invested on earth renders in heaven.

Peter asked Jesus: "We've given up everything to follow you. What will we get?" (Matthew 19:27, NLT). Basically, Peter had his sights on payday. Remember, Christ hadn't been crucified yet, so don't judge Peter's audacity too much.

Jesus answered Peter's question with remarkable love and assurance. It's the same love and assurance He wants you to receive as you count the cost in the twenty-first-century mission field of cyberspace. He said:

*"I assure you that when the world is made new
and the Son of Man sits upon his glorious throne,
you who have been my followers will also sit on twelve thrones,
judging the twelve tribes of Israel. And everyone who has given up
houses or brothers or sisters or father or mother or children
or property, for my sake, will receive a hundred times as much
in return and will inherit eternal life."*
Matthew 19:28–29, NLT

⊍ download

- ↻ **The gift of salvation is priceless.**
- ↻ **The cost is nothing compared to the reward.**
- ↻ **You are either hot—or not what He has called you to be.**
- ↻ **You can count on adversity, so when it shows up, rejoice in it.**
- ↻ **You will grow as you continue to "go" toward the life He's called you to.**

⋒ upload

Dear Lord,

You are Jehovah-Yahweh, the God of my salvation. You are the bridge that allows sinful feet to cross into Your holy presence. You've ransomed me, rescued me, and redeemed me from my broken self. There is no cost too great, no calling too difficult, and no land too treacherous for me to travel in the telling of the things You've done. I submit my online time into Your hands today and ask that You sanctify that time for Your service. Like David, I beg You to shield me from my enemies online as I live out my devotion to You. Be my shield, be my guide, and be my Lord today and always. Amen.

file 11 demystifying: Facebook

@stickyJesus You are a friend of Mine.

Share

Facebook is the number one social networking tool on the Internet, with five hundred million (and growing) registered users, as of this writing. The average user has 130 friends, and users spend more than five hundred *billion* minutes per month on Facebook.

Facebook is one of the most powerful ways to connect with others and share your faith online. If you want to know what the world is thinking, you don't need to guess. That's because the average Facebook user creates seventy pieces of content each month. Facebook users post more than thirty billion pieces of content each month, including Web links, news, stories, blogs, notes, updates, and photos.[1]

features	benefits
Easy registration	You don't need to be tech savvy to begin.
Privacy settings	You maintain control of who has access to what on your Facebook page.
Confirmation of all "friends"	You can add or delete friends anytime.
Profile sections	You can share as much about yourself as you wish.
Content sharing	You can share photos, links, videos, and other content you love with family and friends as well as have them stored for your own reference and enjoyment.
Free application	There are many applications that you can download and use that will add to the value and enjoyment you have while using your site and will enable you to connect via other mobile and electronic devices.

the Christ-centered perspective

In the spirit of summary, if you think you don't have the time to connect with other people on social networks, can't figure it out, or don't see the point—think again. Reaching out to others online is a Kingdom investment that will have Kingdom returns that you can't begin to calculate. This platform allows you a very unique opportunity to keep in daily contact with family, business associates, and childhood, high school, and college friends. Because this social media site can be the most selective in nature, you can keep it as intimate as you desire.

Facebook is a perfect place for you to begin to work out your expression of faith online. Shine His light within your inner circle by reaching out to the people you already know in real life. Use this platform to reach them in a deeper, more personal way. Facebook will help you track the ups and downs of your friends' days. You can be there with them in a way not possible outside this unique social network.

Here's what God's Word says about reaching out to the people around us:

"Love your neighbor as yourself."
Matthew 22:39, NIV

Likely, your "neighbor" is among the nearly two million people logged on the Internet every day. It's hard to love and serve from afar. Many people talking about this new digital mission field will issue the option that reaching out to others online to share the gospel "isn't for everyone." We disagree.

Social networks—if you really look at and consider the numbers—will soon become lifestyle tools as necessary as driving. Most people have grasped the efficiency of driving over walking. It's our educated projection that the same will happen with the Internet's role in daily life.

While we are not cheerleaders for social media, we do believe that we are to be "ready at all times." We can't be ready to give an answer to the world for our faith if the room where we are speaking is empty.

"Always be prepared to give an answer to everyone who asks you to give the reason for the hope that you have."
1 Peter 3:15, NIV

It's often easy for believers to socialize, work, serve, and even vacation with other believers. It's nice. It's safe. Meanwhile, the people just a click away may be struggling or looking for genuine relationship and deeper meaning to life. Perhaps that is why so many seek connection each day through Facebook and other online connection points.

Facebook has become an indispensable prayer chain, coordination tool, and communication channel for churches everywhere. It stands to reason: many people spending an inordinate amount of time online aren't finding that connection in their families, in their jobs, and in some cases (sadly) even their churches.

It's time to spread out and spread the good news on Facebook, beloved.

Chances are, you may already have a Facebook account. But if you don't, here's a Facebook 101 to get you going.

getting started 101

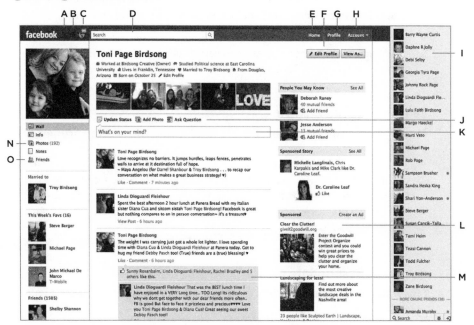

A) Friend requests B) Inbox C) New requests, messages, and notifications D) Friends/groups/event search E) Home page F) Edit profile G) Profile page H) Account admin., change profile settings, help, log out I) Live chat (optional) J) Attach media to your post K) Type your status update here L) Rotating advertisements M) Comments to your status update N) Your photos/change profile picture O) Friends list.

1. **go to http://www.facebook.com/ to open your account**

   ✓ Click on the "Register" link, fill in your information, and agree to the Terms of Use and Privacy Policy.

   ✓ Next, confirm your e-mail address. Facebook will send a confirmation e-mail with instructions on how to set up your account.

   ✓ The Facebook program will guide you through the setup of your home page.

2. **fill out your profile**

   The profile boxes are important because they help you find common ground with others.

   ✓ Click "Profile" on the blue bar across the top of the page.

   ✓ Click "Edit My Profile" option located beneath the place your photo will go once you are in your account.

   ✓ Follow the steps in the "Edit" tool to fill out any information you would like people in your network, or people you accept as friends, to view. It's important to be real here. Don't try to be someone you are not.

   ✓ Complete the profile section with as much detail as you feel comfortable, and click "Save" when you are finished. You can add to or edit your profile at any time.

3. **choose a profile picture**

   This is a very important step. People want to see you, not the profile icon.

   ✓ Select a friendly, welcoming photo of yourself. The fastest way to upload your photo is to use one already in your computer. You can browse computer picture files from Facebook. In time you will find many ways to access new pictures of yourself or other photos that reflect who you are and what you love.

4. **post your first update to your wall**

   The wall is the center of your profile where all the action takes place.

   ✓ Click on your status box (the one that says "What's on Your Mind?"). This is located at the center of the page. The wall is where your friends see your updated status, photos, videos, thoughts, and anything else that you decide to add. Your friends can post comments to your wall, and you can post comments back to their wall, which is called "wall-to-wall." Have fun when you post. Show your hand and let people inside your day with thoughtful reflections and positive comments.

✓ Type something in your status update, and click the "Share" button so the post is saved and published to your wall. Start with what you are doing or thinking. As you watch others, you will develop your voice and what is most interesting to your family of friends.

5. **find and invite friends**

   Find people already on Facebook using the search box on the top left of the screen.

   ✓ Type in the name of a friend. A list of names and pictures will come up.

   ✓ Click "Add as Friend" located to the far right of your friend's photo. This will send a request to the person, and soon you will be connected.

   ✓ To find more friends, click on that person's profile and add friends from his or her list of friends. Little by little, your friends list will grow.

Remember, it's not the *quantity* of friends you have on Facebook as much as it is the *quality* of the relationships you maintain. Accumulating a huge number of friends is not a contest so let go of the numbers. For a believer, adding friends is a genuine commitment to helping others find God's best for their lives. Each time you add a friend, commit to being open to praying for, listening to, engaging with, and loving that person as God puts his or her needs in front of you. Once you jump in, you will have fun exploring all the ways you can connect with others. Facebook is extremely intuitive, and the designers often update its functionality. If you are eager to learn more, we have a list of our favorite books and resources for the emerging tech in you.

a deeper dive

❖ **http://www.facebook.com/**—This is always the best place to start. If you go to your "Account" setting to the far right of the top of your page, you'll find "Help Center" in the drop-down menu. Click and you are on your way!

❖ **http://blog.facebook.com/**—Facebook has a blog loaded with helpful stories, news, and updates.

❖ **the Facebook fan page**—The Facebook fan page is a wonderful resource for how to do most anything on Facebook—lots of insider tips and tricks. You can find it by clicking on "About" located at the lower bottom right corner of any page.

❖ **http://www.gcflearnfree.org/**—This site is great if you prefer watching video tutorials. You can also sign up and click through the non-video tutorials on the site.

❖ **http://www.ehow.com/**—Facebook video tutorials are a key feature provided on this Web site.

❖ **http://www.dummies.com/**—Here you will find the online version of the famous line of how-to books (no, the books are not for dumb people—so explore this site with confidence! The "dummies" brand is an excellent resource for anyone). It has a well-developed library for social media Web sites.

file 12 demystifying: Twitter

> @**stickyJesus** Let your words be few.

Chances are, you've heard the word *Twitter* way too many times. You've waved it off like a gnat, hoping it would go away. You've rolled it around in your head. And when no one was around, you actually said it three times really, really fast. So what in the world is Twitter?

Twitter is an instant messaging service that allows you to send text messages up to 140 characters in length to a list of followers. It is often referred to as microblogging too.

at a glance

- ❖ Twitter has 200 million registered users.

- ❖ Each day 460,000 new users sign up.

- ❖ 110 million tweets are posted each day.

- ❖ Sixty percent of all tweets come from third-party apps.

- ❖ There are 600 million search queries on Twitter per day.

- ❖ There are more than 100,000 Twitter applications.

- ❖ Thirty-seven percent of active Twitter users use their phone to tweet.[1]

All tweets live on a common Web site, http://twitter.com/, and it allows you (and millions of other people) to establish your own page and send short updates alerting your followers to what you're doing, what you're thinking, and what you find interesting. That's it. Really. Big thoughts. Little posts. (Yes, some people do post that they are flossing their teeth or petting their cat, but you don't *have* to follow them!)

features	benefits
Easy registration	You don't need to be tech savvy to begin.
Privacy settings	You can control who sees your tweets.
Instant follow	If you want to follow someone, you can, but if the privacy is set, you may have to wait for his or her approval.
Instant unfollow/block	You can add, delete, or block followers anytime.
Profile sections	There is limited space to describe yourself. Web sites can be added to link people to more about you, your blogs, or your profession. Pictures and avatars can be used to personalize your content feed.
Content sharing	You can share status updates, photos, article links, video links, and other content as long as it is within 140 characters.
Statistics tracking	The side bar provides a navigation system that enables you to track core statistics, public messages, direct messages, retweet activity, and trending topics.

the Christ-centered perspective

It won't take you long to gather that people use Twitter in a variety of ways—as a marketing tool, as e-mail, as conversation among business teams at conferences, and as a texting channel in small groups. It will be easy to jump into the flow of the conversation and find your voice here. You can use the search box on the top of the page to type in key words of topics that interest you. More than likely, you will find a conversation out there that you feel comfortable joining.

Numerous conversations happen 24/7 regarding faith and Christianity. Plugging those key words into the search is fast and easy. By finding these conversations and participating in them, you can learn and be inspired. You can observe how others are keeping it real and living their faith online. Participating in conversations with other believers provides you with solid discipleship training for this mission field.

Twitter is about delivering high impact in a few words. This platform will challenge you to be clear and to the point. It will force you to drop the clutter and focus on your mission. Twitter also allows you to post links to other Web sites, videos, and pictures. With a provocative statement and an attached link, you have the opportunity to bring someone into an experience that could change his or her life for eternity.

getting started 101

A) Find people/topics/hashtags B) Home page view C) Profile view D) Direct messages (DM) E) Suggestions who to follow F) Admin panel G) Your latest post H) People following your feed I) People you follow J) Suggestions who to follow K) Top hashtags on Twitter per day L) Tweets of people you follow M) Lists you create and lists you appear on N) List of searches you've saved O) Twitter activity of people you follow P) @people who have mentioned you Q) Tweets of people you follow R) Put your tweets here.

1. **Go to https://twitter.com/signup**

2. **In the first field fill out your full name**

   ✓ By using your real name, you will connect more easily with your followers.

3.   **next, you will be asked to select a username**

   ✓   Choose a name that describes you—whether it's a nickname, an interest or a hobby. For example @stickyJesus.

   ✓   You can change your username in account settings at any time. So don't panic if you change your mind.

4.   **in the next field, enter a password**

   ✓   Make sure your password contains letters, numbers, and symbols.

5.   **provide e-mail to confirm your account**

   ✓   Once you have chosen a strong password, provide an e-mail address in the next field. You need this to confirm your account before your account is live.

6.   **next, Twitter will ask you to select some of your interests from the left-hand side of the screen**

   ✓   This will generate suggested accounts you might like to follow. By clicking the "follow" button next to a user's name, you add them to the list of users you are following.

7.   **if you choose, Twitter will scan your e-mail address book for people you know that are also using Twitter**

   ✓   Just type your e-mail address and your e-mail password into the boxes, then hit "Find friends."

   ✓   Soon, you'll see a list of people from your address book. You can choose to follow all of them by selecting the blue "Follow All" button on the right-hand side of the results, or if you'd like to see updates only from specific people, you can choose to ask to follow your e-mail contacts individually using the grey "send request" button next to their information.

8.   **you will see more follow options of people you know who are not on Twitter with a similar option to invite**

   ✓   If you select all your contacts and proceed, it will invite all your contacts.

9.   **the next screen will prompt you to search and follow anyone else on Twitter; this list will be people you don't know but who are suggested by Twitter**

   ✓   You can opt to follow or skip this screen.

10. **after you have searched, surfed, and followed a few more people, click the blue "Next step: you're done!" button to finish your sign up process**

   ✓ This action takes you to your home page—or your timeline—where you can now share information (in 140 characters or less) in the box marked "What's happening?"

twitter lists: how to funnel the flood

We can't say enough about the importance of making Lists on Twitter. Lists are critical in terms of time management, efficiency, and engagement. Lists are other Twitter users who you've collected and categorized into a subgroup for easy tracking. This is especially useful if you have several thousand followers and can only truly engage with your favorite people.

Lists funnel the flood of faces into manageable rivers. Lists are displayed on the right side menu of your homepage. You might create lists such as: Favorite Bloggers, Top Resources, Business, News, Inspiration, Family, Pastors, Church Family, Social Media Pros. When you click on your lists, you will be taken to that grouping of people and be able to see what they are tweeting about and engage with them.

You can make your lists private or public. By locking a "Top Friends" list, other followers can't see the list or access it. By making a list public, anyone can go in and follow your list or the individuals in that list. This is a great way to find targeted people to follow. Twitter allows you to create twenty lists so name your categories wisely.

For easy instructions on how to create a List, go to: http://support .twitter.com/ and click on "Twitter Basics."

twitter lingo

tweet   A tweet is a 140-character message sent to the public TwitterStream via phone, the Web (twitter.com), or a third-party application (such as HootSuite or TweetDeck). Tweets are public with two exceptions: direct tweets and protected tweets.

@name	The @ sign in front of your username is your Twitter handle or ID. This is how people will know you, get your attention, and reply to you in the Twitter stream. Putting the @ first means that only the person the comment is meant for will see it. Your other followers can't see that tweet unless they go to your profile.

This is how your tweet appears:

@stickyJesus Are you being The Vine or a branch today? Just asking. Read John 15:5.

twitterStream	Your TwitterStream is your collection of flowing tweets that appear by the second sent by everyone that follows you.
follow	To follow someone on Twitter means you've found common ground of some kind and now subscribe to their Tweets or updates. You can follow anyone without their approval.
follower	A follower is someone who has chosen to follow your Twitter stream. Your tweets appear in their daily stream.
DM (direct message)	A direct message is a 140-character message that is private. You can send a DM by clicking on anyone's profile and choosing "Direct Message" in the sidebar on your Home page. The person must be following you to send a DM.
RT (retweet)	A retweet is when you read something another Twitter user has shared that rings true with you and might benefit your followers. You can use the retweet button to the right of the person's tweet in your stream (hover over the area).

The best way to structure a RT:

RT @TamiHeim You can never separate a leader's actions from his character. –John Maxwell

Or RT like this:

You can never separate a leader's actions from his character. –John Maxwell (via @TamiHeim)

Add your own comment to a RT:

RT @TamiHeim You can never separate a leader's actions from his character. –John Maxwell

#hashtag

The pound sign (#) before a keyword on Twitter is called a hashtag. A hashtag is an easy and efficient way to group tweets on a specific topic by keyword. It is especially useful for events and groups that want to converse within a specific stream.

Using a hashtag looks like this:

@stickyJesus Praying for physical & spiritual healing 4 the children of Haiti. #prayer #Haiti

or

@stickyJesus Speaker Patsy Clairmont now on stage showing us Proverbs in a whole new light! Could stay here forever! #WOF

(This #WOF hashtag would categorize the conversation between everyone tweeting at the Women of Faith event.)

#FF

#FF stands for Follow Friday. Twitter users often suggest who others should follow on Fridays by adding the hashtag #FF to a tweet that includes their favorite people to follow.

favorite

A favorite is a bookmarked, or saved, tweet. You can store these tweets in a list (that will appear as a collected stream in your sidebar). People can browse your favorites and see thoughts and links that echo your heart or your brand. You can favorite a tweet by clicking on the little star next to it in the twitter stream.

blocking

To block someone on Twitter means they will be unable to follow you or add you to their lists. To block someone, you must go to their page and hit "block" on their sidebar.

tweetUp

A TweetUp is a face-to-face gathering outside of the Twitterverse (Twitter.com) of people who have connected on Twitter. A TweetUp can be two, a few, or a party!

a deeper dive

❖ **http://twitter.com/**—The Twitter help section is packed with the basics to get you rolling on Twitter. Take the time to read. It's a must!

❖ **http://www.youtube.com/**—Go to the search box on YouTube. com and find our favorite "how to" Twitter videos there: Twitter in Plain English, Getting Started with Twitter, Twitter Lists in a Nutshell, Top Twitter Tools Exposed and Explained, Finding Followers, and How to Tweet from Any Cell Phone.

❖ **http://mashable.com/**—Just type what you are looking for in the search box.

❖ **http://twittercism.com/**—Type into the search box anything you want to know about how to use Twitter.

❖ **http://howto.wired.com/wiki/main_page/**—The Wired How To Wiki is packed with tutorials on everything social media related. Type your term into the search box.

> **@stickyJesus** Because you believe, you speak.

Blogging has carved a valuable place for itself as a powerhouse communication tool. For some, blogging has become a digital pulpit that draws more attendance on any given day than many churches draw on a Sunday. That captive audience spans the globe.

A blog, short for *Weblog*, is a personal journal updated frequently and shared with the public. The blog format is usually a series of written, audio, pictorial, or video entries posted to a single page, often displayed in reverse chronological order. A blog can be part of a larger Web site that helps a company, an organization, or a church connect deeper with its audience.

Blogs generally echo the personality of the author, church, or company. Blog topics are as varied as the people who write them and represent everything from politics to religion, art, cooking, and business. The authors (bloggers) are endless in their interests, personalities, and writing styles. Bloggers mix photos, breaking or timely news, art, music, and other postings to enhance the blog topic and help it stand out in the crowded blogging world.

Blogs are ideal if you are passionate about a topic, an idea, or a personal philosophy. Not confined to any magic word count, blogs allow you to go deeper into a topic, build relationship, and establish your own library of copyrighted content, which you can then feed to your other social networking sites to strengthen your reach and influence (for Christ) online.

features	benefits
Easy setup	You don't need to be a tech head to launch a blog.
Daily posts	Post what you want, when you want, at any word count you want. Go deeper into your topic, interact with others, and establish your own library of content.
Comments	You write. Readers react by posting comments. Comments launch the conversation, allow feedback, and amp your personal connection with others.
Moderator settings	You control comments before they appear on your page.
Share widgets	Make your blog shareable to social networks such as Facebook, Twitter, StumbleUpon, and other social bookmarking sites.
Tags	You can call out or "tag" keywords related to your post or page. This provides alternate navigation routes to your blog for people and search engines. Tags also enable you to categorize posts for archiving.
Permalinks	A permalink connects to a specific article outside your blog. Embedding links into your daily posts will help establish you as an expert, create a larger topic-specific network, and build your personal network with other bloggers.
Notifications	Most blog platforms have a special page that notifies readers of any follow-ups to their comment so a conversation can keep going and going and going...
RSS feed	The RSS feed allows readers to subscribe easily to your daily blog feed (get this function via Feedburner). Make sure your RSS feed button is easy to find.

the Christ-centered perspective

Since the gospel is the stickiest story ever told, committing to write a blog is one of the most powerful channels to get that story heard.

Brian Bailey, author of *The Blogging Church*, says the case for Christian bloggers comes down to one point: "Blogging is simply a new way of telling stories. In the same way that we seek out new modes of worshipping, preaching and reaching out, we must find new methods of sharing stories. The message doesn't change when the methodology changes. If the methodology fails to change, however, we begin to distance ourselves from the people we are called to reach, and we risk becoming irrelevant."[1]

getting started 101

This section could get very technical very fast because of all the options that go into signing up for and starting your blog. Blog choices, looks, gadgets, and platform preferences are as varied as the people writing them. Overwhelming you is not the goal. We've narrowed this 101 down to two platforms.

1. **choose a blogging platform such as WordPress (http://wordpress.com/) or blogger (http://www.blogger.com/)**

   ✓ Choose a hosted or self-hosted site. Google the pros and cons of each.

   ✓ Each platform will walk you through a "Create a Blog" section that's really easy.

   ✓ Choose a domain name; the shorter the name, the easier it is to memorize.

2. **design your blog**

   ✓ Don't stress over having the best blog design at this stage. Sites like WordPress.com have thousands of template designs for sale and for free that are pretty intuitive to implement.

3. **plug in your tools — be social**

   ✓ Be sure to socially amp your blog! This means, add plug-ins that make it a breeze for visitors to post your daily content to Facebook, Twitter, Google+ and other social sites. Tools and plugins make any blog sing. Just a few to consider: Feedburner (delivers RSS content to a reader), Facebook Connect (integrates FB into your blog), Google Analytics (has free stats for your blog), stat counter (is another great tool for stats), and WP Database Backup Plugin (backs up your core database). You can learn more about your options by Googling "blog tools." Add content slowly, and add what is relevant to your audience. Don't get so fixed on tools that you neglect your daily posts.

4.   use available resources

✓   Go to http://www.blogger.com/ and find "Features." This will lead you to the many ways to amp your blog. WordPress.com has the same support on its "Support" page. Both have a Q&A board where you can ask a question and get an answer. Easy! Both are also adding to their features daily, so be prepared to go deep and have a blast revving up your skills. For a step-by-step visual process to doing anything in your blog, we love eHow.com. Just type what you are looking for in the search box and you are on your way!

guiding principles

✓   Develop a writing style and tone appropriate to your subject material. Practice. You'll find your wings in time.

✓   Study the same kinds of blogs once you choose your topic. Decide what you like and don't like and what you can do differently to stand out.

✓   Post often, even if your posts are short. Some people post daily. You should post at least two, if not three, times a week to let people know you are serious and can be a source of great information.

✓   Write compelling, fun headlines that translate well and gain attention on your Facebook and Twitter feeds. They will prompt visits to your blog.

✓   Keep it real. Few people online are looking for a thesis review. People love blogs because they are *conversational*. Write to your readers like you would talk to your friends. The more energetic your posts, the more interested your readers will be. Try this: get a picture in your mind of a good friend. Reveal your real self the way you would to that person—write in the same tone and use the same humor.

✓   Allow your readers to comment on your posts—yes, even comments that blast your opinion. Tolerance is key in sharing your faith. Listening shows respect, and keeping a negative comment on your page shows courage and conviction in what you believe.

✓   Visit and support other blogs to keep your learning fresh and your perspective in shape. You will see a "reader" community emerge as well as a fellow "blogger" community. Both are opportunities.

- ✓ Interact every chance you get; blogging is social. Link to other blogs, respond to comments, be encouraging, and have a good time.

- ✓ Graduate to adding podcasts, a photo library, or video casts.

- ✓ As much as you are aching to write—take the time to read. Keep your knowledge and perspective fresh so when people read your writing, there's a tone of growth and vision running through it.

- ✓ Write a mission statement for your blog. It's tempting to get off course or respond emotionally to a circumstance in your life that has nothing to do with your blog. Do this random dance too often, and people will stop dropping by.

a deeper dive

- ❖ **Problogger** (http://www.problogger.net/)—This blog educates new bloggers from A to Z. Check out the archives section for tips and tricks to get started.

- ❖ *Blogging for Dummies* (http://www.amazon.com/)—If you have no idea how to start a blog or what to blog about, you can't find a better book than this. It has everything you need to know to get going. Also, go to http://dummies.com and type "blogging" into the search box. You'll find videos, cheat sheets, and tips galore.

- ❖ **About.com** (http://www.about.com/)—Type "blogging" into the search box. You'll find tons of great info.

demystifying: content gathering

Share

So where in the world do I get fresh, interesting content to share every day?
Great question. The fear of coming up empty is a common one. Even the most prolific writers can struggle to keep people hooked on what they have to say as a way of building relationships online. However, as we learned in File 5, you follow the King of Content, which means you draw from a very deep well.

To become adept in social networking for the long haul, initially, you'll need to hunt for the kind of information you want to share. You need to track down a powerful, reliable list of online resources (links, videos, photos, publications, webzines, podcasts, blogs) that echo and strengthen your message. If you are not an avid reader, you will become one soon.

You will need to surf, read, discern, and gather. Take your time as you create a library of information sources, news, and biblically-based resources that personally resonate with you.

To help you get started on content harvesting, we're going to demystify RSS feeders and RSS readers (aggregators) and touch on social bookmarking. These tools will open up an exciting and endless landscape of content, learning, and sharing to you.

A big reason why the Web has become so social can be attributed to a sweet little technology called RSS (Really Simple Syndication or Rich Site Summary). We want you to become an RSS user (it's legal—don't worry). Let's say you visit ten of your favorite blogs or devotionals every day. Once you are there, you click around, read a little, snag a few articles, and cut and paste them into a Word doc to save and then you leave the site. But first you bookmark that page so you can go back. The next day you do the same thing on the same ten blogs. Soon, you're kicking yourself about how much time you've spent online.

RSS technology (attached to most sites) allows you to literally feed all your favorite sites onto one RSS reader, which is kind of like a virtual bookshelf customized with only your choice of books. RSS replaces "seeking" content with content "delivery." It is a great tool for avid readers, researchers, pastors, ministry leaders, parents, or professionals who want to stay current or be constantly "fed" the latest and greatest. Or for you as you seek to share powerful content online.

Almost every Web site or blog you visit today will have this button on it, which is an RSS feed button. That means the content of the site can  be delivered straight to your RSS reader each time that content is updated. (For those of you who are getting this, the world just stretched and will never go back to its original shape!) RSS feeds are free and will "push" information daily to your RSS reader, sometimes called a news aggregator. *Aggregator* is a scary word that sounds like it has sharp teeth, but all it means is "a collector of information." We want to pull the World Wide Web into a funnel that is customized just for you and your interests. We want to tame the beast because it's getting larger by the minute. The goal is to be as productive as possible when you are online and turn the flood into a stream. RSS (the aggregator) helps you do that in one updated interface that you can read anytime. Funneling what you need is not only efficient; it's completely empowering as you live more and more online.

When you get the bulk of a site's content pushed to your reader, it will show up in raw form, void of all the bells and whistles (buttons and ads) of a Web site, which can be a great thing if you love to take in pure information. You can flag articles in your RSS reader to send to a friend or, in the context of this book, to tweet, facebook, e-mail, or share on your blog as a way to start a lively discussion or add value to the mix. Most RSS feeds also push videos, photos, and so on, which can be shared.

popular rss readers include the following:

❖ **Google Reader**	http://www.google.com/reader/
❖ **Bloglines**	http://bloglines.com/
❖ **NewsGator**	http://www.newsgator.com/

Note: RSS readers can be Web-based or desktop. A Web-based reader allows you to read RSS feeds wherever you are. A desktop reader is contained in your computer but can be read off-line. Current versions of Internet Explorer and Firefox also include RSS ability.

view of google reader

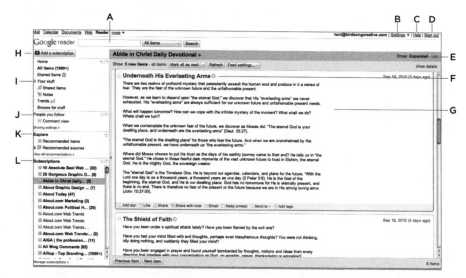

A) Search your reader B) Change your settings C) Help on reading your feed, subscribing, sharing, and organizing (a must read!) D) Sign in/sign out with a Google account E) Change your view. Read list of headlines or article briefs F) Click headline to read full article and retweet, repost, or share G) Article brief H) Cut and Paste URL of favorite sites here to add to reader I) Create your profile for sharing and view favorites J) View your reader community (if you've built one) K) View popular articles and media of the day recommended by others L) View and manage subscriptions.

the Christ-centered perspective

What do you love? Do you love sports? Do you love studying the Bible? Do you love marketing and technology? Do you enjoy history or politics? Are you an advocate for cancer research? Are you into the stock market? Whatever your niche in life, when you join social networks, the goal is to pepper your biblical content with interesting, culturally relevant, humorous, entertaining posts that uniquely bring God's voice into your area of wonderment or expertise. That's everything from a popular YouTube video of a cat playing the drums to a smackdown sermon by T. D. Jakes or an inspiring music video by Michael Gungor. Wherever the Holy Spirit leads you, share it. It's His job to prepare hearts to receive it.

As an ambassador for Christ, you have His content as your content. There are not enough days in your lifetime to exhaust the mysteries, the depth, the heights, or the dimensions of His life-changing, soul-morphing truth.

"You are a chosen generation, a royal priesthood, a holy nation,
His own special people, that you may proclaim the praises of Him
who called you out of darkness into His marvelous light;
who once were not a people but are now the people of God,
who had not obtained mercy but now have obtained mercy."
1 Peter 2:9–10, NKJV

Be mindful not to become the 24/7 Jesus channel in HD. Think about it: if you yammer about one thing all the time at social gatherings, people will eventually see you coming and promptly go (or run) the other way. The same holds true in a social networking environment. Speak to people online the way you would face-to-face. Become known as the person in the room adding value, listening, responding appropriately, and having a great time doing it.

automatic updates

The beauty of an aggregator is that it not only grabs and tags your favorite Web sites and blogs; it also *updates* your subscriptions hourly and can be shared between aggregator users, which makes it social (talk about multiple levels of connection!).

Each aggregator is slightly different from the next in the kinds of sites it aggregates, but for ease at the "get started" level, we'll focus on **Google Reader**.

1. to set up google reader, go to http://www.google.com/

✓ Navigate to the Google home page. At the top left of the screen you will see some options. Click on the "More" button. When that tab drops down, select "Reader."

✓ Next, look for the sign-in box, and click on the "Create an Account Now."

✓ This is not creating a Gmail account. You can use any existing e-mail account, and this will also allow you to access a range of other Google services.

✓ The next screen tells you that Google has sent you an e-mail with a verification link. Look for that e-mail and click on the link. You will be taken to a new screen that says your e-mail address has been verified. Click on the link to manage your account profile.

✓ Look for the "My Services" section on the right. Click on the "Reader" link.

✓ Congratulations: you have now signed up for Google Reader.

2. add subscriptions to your reader

✓ Look for the button icon on the top left-hand side that says "+Add Subscription." When you click on this, you will get a box to add a Web site address.

✓ Here you can do a few things. Enter the URL (Web address) of the Web site that you'd like to subscribe to, and the reader should automatically detect the feed.

✓ Or you can click on the "Discover" button and search for a keyword.

✓ When you locate the correct feed, click the "Subscribe" button.

✓ The latest posts will appear in your reader in the right-hand column. Soon, your reader will replace all your surf time.

3. go to sites and add them to your reader

✓ One of the easiest ways to subscribe to feeds is when you're actually on the Web site that you want to subscribe to. Most blogs will have an RSS icon. There are varied formats, but usually they look something like this:

✓ Clicking on this button on a Web page will often bring up a page of options of readers like this:

✓ Simply click on the "Add to Google" icon. It will then feed to your reader.

✓ Don't panic if you see a page that contains code that makes little sense when you click the orange RSS button. Simply add (cut and paste) the URL (box at the very top of a Web page that's really long) to the RSS reader. The RSS reader will translate the code and display the feed's content in a format that is easily readable.

That's really all there is to it. Once in your Google Reader, you can click on the "Help" button all the way at the top right of the page, and you will have access to in-depth instruction on your reader including:

✓ Getting Started Guide, which is a step-by-step visual guide to everything you need to know about your screen and what it means

✓ Understanding how to discover more feeds, share your feeds, and add comments and notes

✓ Organizing your feeds

✓ Learning shortcuts, tips, and tricks to maximizing your reader

fill up your reader

Now try out your RSS buttons! There's a ton of great Christian content on the Web, and we will be updating and sharing our favorites on http://www.stickyJesus.com/. A simple search today will get you started. Ask Google, "What are the top Christian blogs?" and you will discover many sites full of lists, rankings, and recommendations. There are many new sites you will want to explore. Once you find the ones you like, you can easily add them to your feed.

social bookmarking

A step beyond RSS is social bookmarking. Social bookmarking is tagging (using a word to describe an article or Web site) and saving it in an online database to be referenced at a later date. Instead of saving, or bookmarking, articles to your Web browser, social bookmarking to sites such as digg, StumbleUpon, deli.ci.ous, or reddit allows you to save items to the Web. Again, because your bookmarks are Web-based, they are "social," meaning you can easily share them with friends. You will discover people who share your love for Thai cooking, the Pauline epistles, or stargazing—yes, many communities of like minds exist layers into the Web. And by tagging and sharing, you are gaining twice the knowledge with half the work as you try to wrangle all the information on the Web. So, what began as just keeping tagged lists of articles has morphed into mini search engines, thanks to the social aspect of sharing. Bloggers attach social bookmarking icons to their posts in hopes that people will bookmark them, share them, and drive traffic to their sites. It has become a powerful way to get great content noticed online.

when in doubt, google it

For all the fancy social ways we connect, don't forget that Google (or Yahoo!) is still a good ol' fashioned (often overlooked) way to get exactly what you are looking for. Do you want to quote a favorite author? Need some inspiring Scriptures fast? Looking for a certain music video? Need a four spiritual laws refresher course? How about funny one-liners or jokes to lift your day? Just Google it. Try it: "Scriptures on forgiveness," "quotes and friendship," "clean jokes," "Tozer quotes," or "Spurgeon devotional." This will give you great content at your fingertips. Don't forget to use social bookmarks so you don't have to waste time searching again for your favorite resources. For more advanced searches, go to your Google page, and click the small "Advanced Search" next to the main Google search box. Or on the main Google page, below the main box, click "About Google." From there, under the first header "Our Products," click "Help." On the next page, click "Web Search Help" and "Basic Search Help." This will take you to a page that will give you every combination of search terms and symbols to help you dig through Google like a pro.

a deeper dive

❖ **http://www.youtube.com/**—Once there, type into the search box any of these: "RSS in Plain English," "Google Reader in Plain English," "Social Bookmarking in Plain English." This video gives you an overarching visual on the logic of these topics, and it will give you a great walk-through of each. Makes it fun and easy!

❖ **http://www.ehow.com/, http://www.about.com/**—Just type any of the topics we've mentioned ("RSS feeds") in the search box. You'll find written and visual overviews of everything you need to know to get rolling.

you: a witness

> **@stickyJesus** Tell somebody what I have done for you.

Share

The possibilities for the Kingdom in the online world are real, they're here, and they're now. The invitation exists for anyone with access to the Internet. Transformation has started, and you are here to be part of it. The testimonies of grace, forgiveness, redemption, and new life are echoing through cyberspace—if you listen. What was true in the day of Jesus has only compounded in the time since He walked this earth.

"Jesus did many other things as well.
If all of them were recorded,
I imagine the world itself wouldn't have enough room
for the scrolls that would be written."
John 21:25, CEB

gordon's story

Profile: Gordon Marcy is a Christ follower, digital scribe, and currently working with a team to create the first Internet television syndication network for the Christian broadcast industry.

Tools: Twitter, Facebook, website, blog, LinkedIn, social bookmarks

Links: Follow Gordon at @GordonMarcy, read his blog at www.gordonmarcy.com

Through a network of blogs and social networking sites (and divine appointment), I have been able to meet and interact with people I would likely have never met off-line. All of us have found one another through our common interest in leveraging technology to spread the gospel. Forming these relationships through digital channels has been an exceptional, exciting experience. But nothing prepared me for the Great Commission potential of the new Internet evangelism platforms such as Global Media Outreach (GMO).

Since its inception in 2004, GMO (www.globalmediaoutreach.com) has seen the number of people indicating a decision for Christ through its Internet platform grow from 21,066 annually to a staggering 15,507,537 people in 2010.

More than 2,468,662 of those people voluntarily asked for additional follow-up from one of the nearly 6,000 Christians that have become online missionaries.

If Internet evangelism was truly a part of God's last days movement, I didn't want to be left out the action, so I joined the online movement.

The most surprising and awe-inspiring aspect of online ministry is that relationships can go very deep, very fast.

I first heard from Dembe* in Uganda on March 3, 2011. He e-mailed to say that he had recommitted his life to Jesus. I wrote back to let him know that it was great to be his brother in Christ. And that I was available to pray with him and to answer questions about his spiritual journey.

About 30 percent write back.

Dembe wrote again: "It's nice to hear from you. Actually I have a couple of things I would like you to pray for me. Firstly, I have been an addict to porn and sexual impurity with evil thoughts, so I need serious deliverance prayers. I have been in ministry while sinning. What I want is a renewed relationship with Jesus and a return to ministry with no attachment to sin. You can't imagine. I have lost jobs and favor because of this, but I thank Jesus for bringing me back home."

Dembe's openness and honesty moved me. I then asked God to help me ratchet-up a worthy spiritual response. I wanted Dembe to know he was not alone.

I wrote out a prayer and shared 1 Peter 5:9. "Stand firm against the devil, and be strong in your faith. Remember that your Christian brothers and sisters all over the world are going through the same kind of suffering."

Dembe continued to write asking for prayer, hope, and inspiration. So I committed to pray for him daily for an entire week. That day I happened to see a Twitter post about a pastor's story of porn addiction and redemption. I sent the link to Dembe, and prayed that we would both have faith in the great unseen power—Jesus Christ.

A holy life is a mighty struggle. But would the Spirit work through the faith and prayers of two brothers, 6,000 miles apart, who linked lives only by technology?

On August 25, the answer arrived.

Dembe wrote: "I am realizing changes in my life. I really thank God for you. I can now spend a month without porn. I am getting better. I surely know my Redeemer lives and will completely save me. You may not realize what you mean to me with the inspiration, but God who watches will reward you for your patience, generosity, and love. Thank you very much for the prayers. I am attending a cell [small group] gathering and things are getting better. Through your prayers the Lord is doing much in me. Stay blessed all the days of your life. Keep on with that good heart and with the ministry. It has helped me improve."

The online world is inhabited by millions of seekers like Dembe. There are many who have not heard or understood that Jesus is their Savior; there are those with questions, those looking for hope, those wanting biblical wisdom, and those wanting to obey the Lord.

We are the first generation—ever—to hold in our hands the technology to give every one of them multiple chances to accept Jesus and to follow Him completely.

Is God prompting you to join in the fight to win souls online? I pray that He is.

richie's story

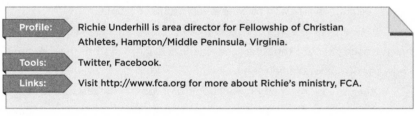

Profile:	Richie Underhill is area director for Fellowship of Christian Athletes, Hampton/Middle Peninsula, Virginia.
Tools:	Twitter, Facebook.
Links:	Visit http://www.fca.org for more about Richie's ministry, FCA.

* Names have been changed.

Jesus said in the gospel of Matthew to make disciples as you go about your everyday life. If you move about online with that mind-set, every encounter begins to look quite different.

When I created an account on Facebook, as a pastor, I immediately realized the possibilities of ministry. I was able to see faces, words, updates...and a field white for harvest. God had put people in my path from my past and my present and had allowed me incredible—and what I viewed as divine—access into so many remarkable hearts and minds. Some people see mere updates, tweets, or posts, but I see something entirely different.

For months I loved getting reacquainted, listening, and responding to old and new friends. After several months of building and rebuilding relationships online, someone I had known in high school posted a very dark, ominous statement in her status update. Having served as a corporate chaplain for eight years, I knew this situation could get very serious, very quickly. So I immediately sent her a private message on Facebook and put in the subject line: "Help is on the way." I then wrote in the body of the message: "Hey, Katie,* call me anytime...I mean it...I have a lot of experience dealing with these issues...take me up on my offer!!"

She responded within an hour, telling me thanks but I would not understand. She also said that she felt awkward because she had known me in her past and had trouble seeing me as a minister. However, one advantage of online ministry is the ability to express and share a bit more freely and quickly than a face-to-face encounter. In this case, being online was on my side. After some reassuring dialogue, Katie felt safe enough to give me a chance to help her and began to share her situation. She revealed that her husband had recently caught her in multiple cybersex relationships and wanted to end their marriage immediately. She felt her life was over, and she could no longer live with the consequences of her actions. She was in a desperate state of mind. That intense conversation turned into six solid days of dialogue via Facebook direct messages, resulting in renewed hope in a very troubled woman.

By God's grace and a consistently transparent online dialogue, Katie and her husband are still together, and she is making daily progress desiring to know the Savior who died for her.

Other situations arise on Facebook that look fairly casual but evolve to something deeper. Jesus called His followers to be fishers of men, so quite often I go fishing on Facebook. I really do care about the people in my online communities, and I'm constantly looking for ways to share the hope of Christ that possesses my own heart.

One day someone had posted the question in her status update: "If you could wish for anything what it would be?"

A hodgepodge of answers followed the question, but one comment jumped out to me. A woman named Laurel* simply wrote: "purpose."

The God of the universe can use any method He chooses.

Wow. The Holy Spirit was on the move, and it was time to cast a divine line into the Facebook waters. Not wanting to embarrass the woman (I really didn't know her very well) or put her on the spot, I sent her a direct message. I asked if she was serious about her comment. She surprised me with an emphatic "yes!"

I looked for biblical content that I could direct her to that could speak to her very basic need. (This is what you need to do if you don't have the benefit of hours to discuss a biblical topic that goes so much deeper than what you can write in a direct message.) I referred her to Rick Warren's *Purpose Driven Life* Web site (http://www.purposedrivenlife.com/) and told her that I was personally available to be a resource to her.

Her response was positive. After two months of praying for my friend and exchanging messages, Laurel and I eventually had a face-to-face meeting. She brought along her adult son, who also had recently begun his own spiritual journey.

I had the opportunity to share my testimony and to answer a number of their theological and doctrinal questions. I also gave them Lee Strobel's DVD documentary, *The Case for Christ* (http://www.leestrobel.com/), and referred both Laurel and her son to several Web resources including Chip Ingram's Living on the Edge (http://www.livingontheedge.org/).

I recently received a Facebook message from my friend telling me that she was discovering the gifts with which God has entrusted to her and I was immediately "friended" by her son.

Such situations confirm to me that the God of the universe can use any method He chooses—including Facebook—to bring wandering hearts into His loving care.

* Names have been changed.

jamee rae's story 💬

Profile: Jamee Rae Pineda is involved with a Christian recovery ministry that uses ten Bible-based principles to transform lives.

Tools: Twitter, Facebook, Web site, blog.

Links: Follow Jamee at @TheSolidRockRoad, read her blog at http://thesolidrockroad.blogspot.com/, and visit her Web site at http://www.thesolidrockroad.com/.

There's no doubt that God is moving in this new, vast digital realm of the social Web—especially on behalf of ministries and nonprofits. It's so exciting to see how He daily orchestrates conversations and connects lives online, so much so that social networking has become a big part of our team's efforts to get our resources into the hands of people who need it most. We're about helping Christians in addiction, so when people respond to our content, it's clear our time invested online each day is well spent.

While moving within this new frontier, we've learned a lot. We identified our primary target market online, which isn't the addict (the person we wrote our book for) but rather the *family members* of addicts as well as pastors and churches. This was some valuable market research we gained free of charge, which is just one of the beauties of this new and exciting method of marketing.

Recently, one of my Twitter followers, Marissa,* called me through the number she found on our Web site. I was more than happy to take our relationship off-line and just listen to Marissa's heart. We talked quite a while about a family member whose addiction was tearing apart their family. Marissa said she wasn't sure where to turn until she saw the Solid Rock Road in her Twitter stream and noticed I was using *hope* and *addiction* in the same sentence. By the end of our conversation, Marissa ended up ordering multiple copies of our book, *Follow the Solid Rock Road*, so that every member of her family could read it at the same time. She later reported that the book was full of truths and that it helped the sober members of their family realize that they needed to move out of God's way in the addict's recovery journey.

Sharing God's truth online goes way beyond microblogging in 140 characters at a time. When I tweet, post on Facebook, or blog, I know the Holy Spirit

* Names have been changed.

is working through me. I believe He can use 140 characters—or no characters—to achieve His purposes, so I just show up and pay attention to His lead. My countenance is that of a servant of God, so I'm humbled when my words touch, encourage, inspire, and even convict my online community. The goal for a Christ follower online is to communicate the message of freedom in Christ.

In another instance, one of my Twitter followers, Jacquie*, told me about her homeless ministry. She sent me a link to a video in which she had helped a longtime homeless man enter a Gospel Mission in Southern California. The video touched my heart so I sent her a donation and one of my books. She read it and decided that the best place for the book was at the mission. To know that hundreds and maybe even thousands of people will read our book—people who truly need to understand the power of God—blesses me beyond words. That's why I use social media daily.

> *The goal is to communicate the message of freedom in Christ.*

My counsel to newcomers to this seemingly noisy realm is to be yourself, listen, and not be afraid to connect to total strangers. If you are a believer or part of a ministry, there are people online everywhere who need what you have—it's not much different than walking down a busy street. The approach of the Solid Rock Road team is to answer questions and acknowledge every retweet, comment, and mention. This genuine attention to our circle of friends has resulted in many relationships that have moved from cyberspace to e-mails and phone calls. We also follow everyone who follows us unless the Twitter stream or related Web site is offensive or sexual.

There are three of us on the Solid Rock team who tweet from three different accounts. One day we were blessed by a follower who retweeted each of us every time we provided a link to our Web site and book. She connected wholeheartedly with what we were trying to do online, and she virtually came up beside us to help spread the gospel. That, to me, is the body of Christ.

For a free ministry like the Solid Rock Road, costly promotional campaigns have never been an option. Between our Twitter account, Facebook fan page, blog, and Web site, our message's reach has grown exponentially from a small region in Oregon to reaching around the globe. To do this, we've been intentional about getting our content out there. We created a community of

* Names have been changed.

like-minded believers online, many of whom are now making plans to incorporate our recovery method into their church programs. We've also been intentional about connecting to, caring for, and serving those in our communities. The result is an interactive network of people, all working in unity to further the Kingdom of God throughout the earth. And isn't that what it's all about?

As former addicts, we share our stories, but as Christians moving forward on the path of righteousness, we tell people the hard truth. Thanks to social networking, we are finally able to transmit that truth to the masses and share the good news that God makes all things—especially broken things—new.

you are a digital scribe

So, you've learned the tools, read God's perspectives, and heard the stories from others doing it. Now the time has come to write your own sticky story. You are a digital scribe. You are no different than the disciples, evangelists, and great communicators of the gospel who walked the earth before you. No different than Queen Esther, whose knees were shaking before the king; no different than the Apostle Paul or the fire-hearted evangelist Billy Graham who both dove headfirst into their cultures with a message so contrary that shiny, jaded hearts turned inside out. They asked themselves the same questions you must ask yourself today.

❤ questions to ask yourself before you "go"

- ❖ What's my part in God's plan online?
- ❖ What communities is He calling me to?
- ❖ What tools will I use to communicate?
- ❖ What's being said here?
- ❖ Where's the common ground?
- ❖ What are the needs around me?
- ❖ What's the cultural value here and how can I apply God's truth?
- ❖ How will I respond to temptation?
- ❖ How will I prepare my heart?
- ❖ How will I respond to attacks?
- ❖ Will I play it safe or will I speak?

*"If you keep quiet at a time like this,
God will deliver the Jews from some other source, but
you and your relatives will die;
what's more, who can say but that God has brought
you into the palace for just such a time as this?"*
Esther 4:14, TLB

As she reads the warning note from Mordechai, Queen Esther is crystal clear about the stakes. She gets that God has granted her astonishing influence for this moment in time. If she takes action and speaks to the king on behalf of the Jewish people, they may live—even if speaking out of turn to the King could cost Esther her life. If she keeps quiet, the Jews may perish.

Just as it was true for Esther, it is true for you today. The stakes in front of you as a follower of Christ online are also high—higher, in fact, than they've been in recent history. The world is moving and morphing at warp speed and the meaningless, dead-end chatter and enemy-crafted banter is piling up online like rush-hour traffic. Christ is being discarded. Biblical values are being marginalized more and more. Influence is the currency, and increasingly, Christians are broke. If you choose to roam aimlessly and blend into the online world, some may perish—eternally.

This book doesn't seek to push you online. Studies show that Christians are already there, shiny gadgets in hand. It is however, a wake-up call prompting you to get intentional about *how you spend your time* online— connecting, serving, and leading the conversation in such a way that others will seek to know Christ personally.

So this is it, believer: a moment in history in which your life is center stage for all to consider. Your individual reach is exponentially the most powerful it's ever been. Take heart, look around; you are far from alone. There are many, many, many, many others drawing near with the same spirit and mission. You will easily find them when you start getting intentional online and they will strengthen you.

It's time to link arms and light up the online space for the fame—and the name—of Jesus Christ. And by the way, as you commit to the mission at hand, we will always be right here with you at http://www.stickyJesus.com/, living sticky—one post, one promise, and one prayer at a time.

↻ The Final Download
a Christ follower's stand on social media

↻ my heart

↻ I am on my face before God before I get on Facebook and seek Him before I tweet.

↻ I ask for the Holy Spirit's guidance and discernment before I enter into social media platforms.

↻ I am deliberate about preparing my heart to go online and devoted to the larger, eternal mission.

↻ I am others-focused and enter online communities with a desire to serve.

↻ I am intentional about checking my heart for conceit, superiority, prejudice, and judgment.

↻ I am fully present to people when I engage.

↻ I acknowledge that God values every person I encounter online and that beating hearts are behind every picture and post.

↻ I choose to be digitally generous. I retweet, post comments to blogs, follow up on e-mails promptly, and help promote worthy causes online.

↻ my thinking

↻ I am inclusive, not exclusive, as I engage.

↻ I stay abreast of current events and I am sensitive as to how they might impact members of my online communities and the world.

↻ I check and approve all links to videos, slide shows, blogs, and articles from start to finish before I share them.

↻ I properly attribute quotes, articles, and thoughts that are not my own.

↻ I share accurate information and check facts before I retweet or repost. When in doubt, I don't.

↻ I do not use social media as a platform to aggravate political, religious, or social arguments, but as tools to educate, edify, and inform.

↻ I proofread before I post.

↻ I do not write in all caps (the equivalent of yelling).

↻ my words

↻ I am good, kind, and true in all that I share with others and strive to bring genuine value to my online communities.

↻ I am a faithful, accurate source of the Scriptures online.

↻ I share regular insights regarding what God shows me in His Word.

↻ I share God-honoring content such as links to great blogs, videos, articles, news, sermons, and music.

↻ I never publically criticize or correct others.

↻ I do not post an excessive play-by-play of my daily life.

↻ I maintain a sense of humor and do not take myself too seriously.

↻ When I tell someone "I will pray for you," I do.

↻ my actions

↻ I do not text, tweet, Facebook, or check e-mail while driving.

↻ I set time limits and fervently guard my time spent online. I do not allow social media—or shiny gadgets—to replace or diminish my face-to-face time with others.

↻ I am brief, sincere, and focused in my posts.

↻ I do not preach or broadcast information—I engage in conversations.

↻ I never respond out of impulse.

↻ I follow anyone as long as they continue to follow me (unless their feeds are offensive).

↻ I respond, thank, and acknowledge others online.

↻ I protect my—and my family's—hearts, eyes, and minds with filtering software on all digital devices and talk candidly with family and friends about the significance of God-honoring values and behaviors online.

⋒ the final upload

Dear Lord,

Here I am. Send me as a flawed but focused messenger of Your truth in this Web-based world. I'm stepping out of the boat, cutting straight through the sea, and heading directly into the fire... knowing You are already there to walk with me. I surrender my online agenda to You. Through Your holy hands, recycle my life as an acceptable vessel for Your glory. Lead me to the fields white with harvest and I will labor there until You come for me. Touch my eyes, remove the scales so quick to overlook, judge, or dismiss the beating, seeking hearts You've appointed to my path. Each one belongs to You; each one ransomed by precious blood.

Sharpen my focus, time, and ability so Your reach increases and Your Kingdom rises up in beauty amid the online debris. I will not forfeit the call or shrink back from this heaven-authored time. I thank You that Your love has ruined me for this world; Your grace has wrecked me for personal glory. Unnerve me. Alarm me. Crush my idols. Pull my pride up from its roots with mighty, merciful hands.

Ignite in me the fire of Paul and pour into me the timing of Esther as I move and breathe online. Clothe me in godly courage. Ready my heart for the supernatural. Touch all of Your faithful ministers online, I pray. Expand their territories and influence so Your sticky message of repentance and grace radically transforms the digital landscape.

I surrender my affections for the things of this world and exchange them for the brilliance of a Kingdom that will not fade. Restore Your glory in this Land of Shiny Things, oh Lord, and start Your work of revival with me. Amen.

@stickyJesus™

how to live out your faith online

keep going, keep growing.

Our website, www.stickyJesus.com is an extension of this book.

Join us to learn more about how to #LiveSticky online. You'll find a collaborative community and learn more about social networking, digital outreach, and discipleship.

- ✓ Subscribe to our blog.

- ✓ Learn from posts on faith, technology, outreach, social media, and culture.

- ✓ Comment and contribute to the daily conversation on the site.

- ✓ Encourage others by sharing your living-sticky stories with us.

- ✓ Sign the online pledge and become part of the Digital Scribe community.

- ✓ Be inspired by devotionals created especially for the Digital Scribe.

- ✓ Explore the resources and tips designed to help you increase impact online.

follow us on twitter:
@stickyJesus
@tonibirdsong
@tamiheim

connect to the @stickyJesus fan page on Facebook!

future sticky releases...

**If you connected with the *@stickyJesus* message,
there's more sticky coming!**

A *@stickyJesus Small Group Field Guide:* Small group study instructs how to organize groups for Kingdom impact online.

B *@stickyJesus Student Field Guide:* Teen edition equips youth how to be responsible and represent Christ online.

C *@stickyJesus Devotional:* Daily readings inspire you to center and align your heart with Christ's before connecting online.

Visit **www.stickyJesus.com** and join the community.

glossary of terms

blog

A type of Web site or part of a Web site. Blogs are usually created and maintained by an individual or a team of people with regular entries of commentary, descriptions of events, or other material, such as graphics or video. These can be highly viral with readers able to share them on a wide variety of social media platforms. Blog can also be used as a verb, meaning "to maintain or add content to a blog."

cloud computing

The cloud is a metaphor for the way data is accessed/stored between users and the web. Cloud computing is any computer file or data—word processing, photo, email, game, video, music, application—uploaded to or downloaded from a Web site.

community

A social network is a group of individuals who interact through specific media, potentially crossing geographical and political boundaries in order to pursue mutual interests or goals. One of the fastest growing types of virtual community is social networking services.

direct message	A simple text or notification sent to an individual or small group that is private or intended for only the specific audience to which it is directed.
e-blast	A digital flyer or announcement distributed through e-mail. An e-blast can be a one-time occurrence or something that is repeatedly sent based on an audience's willingness to receive it.
facebook	A social networking Web site where users can create and customize their own profiles with photos, videos, and information about themselves. Friends, or whoever is designated via a user's privacy settings, can browse the profiles of members and write messages, send messages, or share content from other friends' pages.
flickr	An image and video hosting Web site, Web services site, and online community. It is a popular Web site for users to share and embed personal photographs; the service is widely used by bloggers to host images that they embed in blogs and social media.
google	A multinational Internet search technologies corporation that hosts and develops a number of Internet-based services and products. It generates revenue and profit primarily from advertising through its AdWords program.
google+	A social networking project created by Google. It echoes Facebook in its community, sharing, and posting structure but uses circles, hangouts, and sparks that make community and conversation more easily aggregated.
google chrome	An open source lightweight operating system (OS). It uses one-sixtieth as much hard drive space as Windows 7 and is intended for netbooks or tablet

PCs that access Web-based applications and stored data from remote servers.

iPhone
The iPhone is a line of Internet- and multimedia-enabled phones designed and marketed by Apple Inc.

mySpace
A social networking Web site launched in 2003, owned by Fox Interactive Media. The contents of a MySpace profile are Moods, Blurbs, Blogs, interests section, and other details. It is fully able to upload music and photos and receive comments from other users. It's a favorite social networking niche for many teens and people in the music industry.

netscape
A company specializing in Internet software first launched in 1994, now part of AOL.

ning
An online platform for people to create their own social networks.

plaxo
An online address book and social networking service.

podcast
A series of digital media files (either audio or video) that are released by episode. Files are often downloaded through Web syndication.

seo
An acronym for Search Engine Optimization. It describes the use of various techniques to improve a Web site's ranking in the search engines and thus attract more visitors.

social network
A social structure made of individuals (or organizations) called "nodes," which are tied (connected) by one or more specific types of interdependency, such as friendship, kinship, financial exchange, dislikes, relationships, beliefs, or shared knowledge.

tipping point   The point where building momentum results in a radical shift. The outcome is that a new norm is established.

tumblr   A blogging platform that allows users to post text, images, video, links, quotes, and audio to their tumblelog, a short-form blog. Users are able to follow other users and see their posts together on a single dashboard. Users can "like" or "reblog" posts from other blogs from that single site.

vimeo   A video-centric social networking site (owned by IAC/InterActiveCorp) and launched in November 2004. Users must register to upload content. The site supports embedding, sharing, and video storage, and allows user commenting on each video page.

webcast   A media file distributed over the Internet using streaming media technology to distribute a single content source to many simultaneous listeners/ viewers. A webcast may be distributed live or on demand.

white paper   An authoritative report or guide that typically addresses issues and recommends how to solve them. Frequently used to educate readers and help people make decisions. White papers are most often used in politics and business and for technical subjects.

youTube   The number one video-sharing Web site online today where users can upload and share videos. It was created in February 2005 and sold to Google Inc. in November 2006 for $1.65 billion. It is currently operated as a subsidiary of Google.

notes

file 1

1. "World Internet Usage and Population Statistics," http://www. internetworldstats.com/stats.htm (accessed October 6, 2011).

2. "Barna Technology Study: Social Networking, Online Entertainment and Church Podcasts," Barna Group, http://www.barna.org/ search?q=social+media (accessed August 19, 2010).

3. Combined Internet stats from:

   ❖ Jennifer Van Grove, "Remarkable Stats on the State of the Internet," Mashable, http://mashable.com/2010/02/26/state-of-internet/ (accessed September 5, 2010).

   ❖ Eric Qualman, "Social Media Revolution 2 (Refresh)," http://socialnomics. net/2010/05/05/social-media-revolution-2-refresh/ (accessed September 30, 2010).

   ❖ Jeremiah Owyang's blog, http://www.web-strategist.com/blog/ (accessed September 5, 2010).

   ❖ "Adults on Social Networking Sites, 2005-2009," Pew Internet & American Life Project, http://pewinternet.org/Infographics/Growth-in-Adult-SNS-Use-20052009.aspx (accessed September 5, 2010).

❖ "Social Networks/Blogs Now Account for One in Every Four and a Half Minutes Online," Nielsen Wire, http://blog.nielsen.com/nielsenwire/online_mobile/social-media-accounts-for-22-percent-of-time-online/ (accessed September 5, 2010).

4. Jose Antionio Vargas, "Obama Raises Half a Billion Online," November 20, 2008, http://voices.washingtonpost.com/44/2008/11/obama-raised-half-a-billion-on.html (accessed October 2, 2010).

5. "Incorrect predictions," Wikiquote, http://en.wikiquote.org/wiki/ (accessed Sept. 5, 2010).

6. Thomas L. Friedman, *The World Is Flat: A Brief History of the Twenty-First Century,* (2005; repr. New York: Picador, 2007), 48-49, 195.

7. Seth Godin, *Tribes: We Need You to Lead Us* (Ottawa, ON: Portfolio, 2008), 1-2.

file 2

1. Jesse Rice, *The Church of Facebook: How the Hyperconnected Are Redefining Community,* (Colorado Springs, CO: David C. Cook, 2009), 28.

2. Friedman, *The World Is Flat,* 185.

3. Stephen Baker, "Social Media Will Change Your Business," BusinessWeek, http://www.businessweek.com/bwdaily/dnflash/content/feb2008/db20080219_908252.htm?chan=rss_topDiscussed_ssi_5 (accessed August 19, 2010).

4. Francis A. Schaeffer, *A Francis A. Schaeffer Trilogy: Three Essential Books in One Volume* (Wheaton, IL: Crossway Books, 1990), 270.

5. Wikipedia Contributor, "The Tipping Point," *Wikipedia,* http://en.wikipedia.org/wiki/The_Tipping_Point (accessed August 19, 2010).

6.   Malcom Gladwell, *The Tipping Point: How Little Things Can Make a Big Difference* (New York: Back Bay Books, 2002), 12.

file 4

1.   Emanuel Rosen, *The Anatomy of Buzz: How to Create Word of Mouth Marketing* (New York: Doubleday, 2000), 89.

2.   "The history of word of mouth marketing," The Free Online Library, http://www.thefreelibrary.com The+history+of+word+of+mouth+marketing-a0134908667 (accessed March 12, 2010).

3.   Chris Brogan and Julien Smith, *Trust Agents: Using the Web to Build Influence, Improve Reputation, and Earn Trust.* rev. ed. (New York: Wiley, 2009), xii, 18.

4.   "Stickiness," definition, MarketingTerms.com, http://www.marketing terms.com/dictionary/stickiness/ (accessed September 11, 2010).

5.   "Word of mouth marketing," definition, BusinessDictionary.com, http://www.businessdictionary.com/definition/word-of-mouth-marketing.html (accessed January 2, 2010).

file 5

1.   "World Internet Usage and Population Statistics," Internet World Stats, http://www.internetworldstats.com/stats.htm (accessed October 6, 2011).

2.   "History of the Gold Rush," http://www.historichwy49.com/goldrush.html (accessed October 2, 2010).

3.   Kevin Starr, "Chapter 4: Striking it Rich," in *California: A History,* Modern Library Chronicles (New York: Modern Library, 2007), 78-85.

4. Combined Bible facts from:

   ❖ Wikipedia Contributor, "Chapters and verses of the Bible." *Wikipedia*, http://en.wikipedia.org/wiki/Chapters_and_verses_of_the_Bible (accessed September 11, 2010).

   ❖ Kelli Mahoney, "Fun Bible Facts for Christian Teens By the Numbers," About.com. http://christianteens.about.com/od/understandingyourbible/qt/NumberFacts.htm (accessed September 2, 2010).

   ❖ "Bible Facts and Statistics," Preaching Points, http://www.preachingpoints.com/2008/12/bible-facts-and-statistics/ (accessed March 11, 2010).

5. Mark Silver, "Is Spiritual Business a Contradiction in Terms?" Copyblogger, http://www.copyblogger.com/spiritual-business/ (accessed July 13, 2010).

6. Clyde Francis Lytle, ed., *Leaves of Gold*, 7th ed. (Williamsport, PA: The Coslett Publishing Company, 1958), 46.

file 6

1. "Thumb Culture," definition, PCMag.com, http://www.pcmag.com/encyclopedia_term/0,2542,t=thumb+culture&i=52871,00.asp (accessed August 23, 2010).

2. A.W. Tozer, *Tragedy in the Church* (Camp Hill, PA: Christian Pubns, 1978), 55-56.

3. Francis Chan, *Forgotten God: Reversing Our Tragic Neglect of the Holy Spirit.* new ed. (Colorado Springs, CO: David C. Cook, 2009), 110.

file 7

1. Ruth Shipley, "Socialnomics: It's a People-Driven Economy," Social Media Examiner, http://www.socialmediaexaminer.com/socialnomics-its-a-people-driven-economy/ (accessed October 2, 2010).

2. Sarah Lai Stirland, "The Obama Campaign: A Great Campaign, Or The Greatest?" http://wired.com/threatlevel/200811/the-obama-campa/ (accessed Sept. 11, 2010).

3. "Internet: A New Forum for Proclaiming the Gospel," Message of the Holy Father John Paul II For the 36th World Communications Day. The Vatican.va, http://www.vatican.va/holy_father/john_paul_ii/ messages/communications/documents/hf_jp-ii_mes_20020122_world-communications-day_en.html (accessed October 2, 2010).

4. Carrick Mollenkamp, "Americans Pledge Millions, but Cash Flow Takes Weeks," The Wall Street Journal, January 16, 2010, http://online.wsj.com/article/SB10001424052748704381604575005412610261000.html (accessed June 19, 2010).

5. Samuel Axton, "Nashville Flooding: Twitter and YouTube Tell the Story (video), Mashable, http://mashable.com/2010/05/02/nashville-flooding-video-pics/ (accessed June 30, 2010).

6. John Brandon, "Virtual Church," Ministry Today, http://www.ministrytodaymag.com/index.php/ministry-outreach/innovation/15402-virtual-church (accessed September 11, 2010).

7. Robert Dolezal, Jesus and His Times (Pleasantville, MY: Reader's Digest, 1987), 196.

8. "A History of Evangelism and Mass Media." mkmccarthy.homestead.com/files/A_HISTORY_OF_EVANGELISM_AND_MASS_MEDIA.htm (accessed July 1, 2010).

9. "Evangelism," United States History, http://www.u-s-history.com/pages/h3817.html (accessed February 11, 2010).

10. "Profile: Bill and Vonette Bright, Founders Campus Crusade for Christ International," DeMossNews.com, http://www.demossnewspond.com/ccci/press_kit/vonette_bright_profile (accessed August 22, 2010).

11. Brandon, "Virtual Church," http://www.ministrytodaymag.com/index.php/ministry-outreach/innovation/15402-virtual-church (accessed September 11, 2010).

file 8

1. http://www.charlipickett.com/

2. Kimberly Young, "Internet Addiction: Emergence of a New Clinical Disorder," www.netaddiction.com/articles/newdisorder.pdf (accessed August 1, 2010).

3. Richard N. Ostling, "Researcher tabulated world's believers," http://www.adherents.com/misc/WCE.html (accessed August 23, 2010).

4. John MacArthur, note for Romans 12:2, in *The MacArthur Study Bible: Revised & Updated Edition*, (Waco, TX: Thomas Nelson, 2006), 1684.

5. "What Americans Do Online: Social Media And Games Dominate Activity," nielsenwire, http://www.blog.nielsen.com/nielsenwire/online_mobile/what-americans-do-online-social-media-and-games-dominate-activity/ (accessed August 2, 2010).

6. "What Parents Can Do," National Safety Council. http://www.nsc.org/safety_road/TeenDriving/Pages/WhatParentsCanDo.aspx (accessed March 24, 2010).

7. Combined tips from:
   ❖ "Online Safety Tips," CyberPatrol, http://www.cyberpatrol.com/onlinesafetytips.asp (accessed March 20, 2010).
   ❖ "Internet Monitoring Family Game Plan," InternetSafety.com. http://www.internetsafety.com/internet-monitoring-game-plan.php (accessed Sept. 20, 2010).

file 9

1. Ken Blanchard and Phil Hodges, *Lead Like Jesus: Lessons from the Greatest Leadership Role Model of All Time,* (Nashville, TN: Thomas Nelson, 2005), 39-79.

2. Philip Yancey, *What's So Amazing About Grace?* new ed. (Grand Rapids, MI: Zondervan, 2002), 274.

file 10

1. Dietrich Bonhoeffer, *The Cost of Discipleship*, new ed. (New York: Touchstone, 1995), 43-44.

2. Dietrich Bonhoeffer, *Letters & Papers from Prison*, (New York, Macmillan Publishing Company, 1972), Letter dated July 18, 1944.

3. "Paul Washer—Live For Eternity." (video) GodTube Christian Videos. http://www.godtube.com/featured/video/paul-washer-live-eternity (accessed July 5, 2010).

file 11

1. "Press Room," Facebook, http://www.facebook.com/press/info. php?statistics (accessed October 6, 2011).

file 12

1. "Twitter User Statistics Revealed," *The Huffington Post*, http://www. huffingtonpost.com/2010/04/14/twitter-user-statistics-r_n_537992. html (accessed October 6, 2011).

file 13

1. Brian Bailey and Terry Storch, *The Blogging Church*, (San Francisco, CA: Jossey-Bass, 2007), 169.

about the authors

Toni Birdsong is a partner in Birdsong Creative, a graphics, marketing, and Web firm in Franklin, Tennessee. She's served as a reporter and editor for several newspapers and as a communications specialist for the Walt Disney Company. She's authored more than 2,000 articles and currently provides marketing content and social media strategy for businesses. She lives a blessed life with her husband, Troy and their amazing kids, Zane and Olivia. They worship at Grace Chapel in Leiper's Fork, Tennessee.

Tami Heim is the president and CEO of the Christian Leadership Alliance, headquartered in San Clemente, CA. Her professional career includes executive leadership experience in the technology, marketing, publishing and retail industries. She has served as a partner in The A Group - Brand Development, executive vice president and chief publishing officer for Thomas Nelson Publishers, and as the president of Borders, Inc. Tami and husband, Dale, delight in their daughter, Zoë, son-in-law, Matt and first grandchild expected in 2012. As members of Long Hollow Baptist Church, they're compelled by love to frequently go and serve the orphans living in Jeremie, Haiti.

Toni and Tami met on Twitter.